James O'Dea (www.jamesodea.com) is author of *The Conscious Activist*, *Cultivating Peace* and other acclaimed works. He is a former president of the Institute of Noetic Sciences; Washington, DC, office director of Amnesty International; and CEO of the Seva Foundation. He worked with the Middle East Council of Churches in Beirut and lived in Turkey for five years. He has taught peacebuilding to over 1,000 students in 30 countries. He has also conducted frontline social healing dialogues around the world. A member of the Evolutionary Leaders group and of the Advisory Board of *The Peace Alliance and Kosmos Journal*, he also mentors emerging leaders. James is both an activist and a mystic.

SOUL AWAKENING PRACTICE

Prayer, Contemplation and Action

JAMES O'DEA

Foreword by **Lynne McTaggart**

With contributions by Ervin László,
Michael A Singer, Barbara Marx Hubbard,
Anodea Judith, Kabir Helminski and Mona Polacca

WATKINS
Sharing Wisdom Since
1893

This edition first published in the UK and USA 2017 by
Watkins, an imprint of Watkins Media Limited
19 Cecil Court
London WC2N 4EZ

enquiries@watkinspublishing.com

1 3 5 7 9 10 8 6 4 2

Designed and typeset by JCS Publishing Services Ltd, jcs-publishing.co.uk

Printed and bound in Finland

A CIP record for this book is available from the British Library

ISBN: 978-1-78678-052-2

www.watkinspublishing.com

Meher Baba
Avatar of soul awakening

Acknowledgements

Profound thanks to Kabir Helminski, Anodea Judith, Barbara Marx Hubbard, Ervin László, Mona Polacca and Michael Singer for their powerful contributions to this book and to Lynne McTaggart for her inspired Foreword.

Special thanks to those who immediately saw the power of the Soul Awakening Prayer and to those who have made it a regular part of their spiritual practice –including Cheyenne Mendel, Nico Kladis, Marika Popovits, Nora Tunney, William and Brahmi Howell, and Colleen Hall.

Thanks to my beloved family and dear friends like Michael Singer, Tanja Andrejasic-Weschler, Molly Rowan Leach, Ramloti, Marika Popovits, Burt Wadman, Robin Gurung, Seqouyah Trueblood, Suzanne Eugster and Jacqueline Zoe de Bray for constant nurturing friendship and support during life's darker challenges.

Great thanks to my publisher at Watkins, Jo Lal, for her tireless encouragement and support and to my editor Bob Saxton for his commitment to the heart and soul of this book.

Finally, I acknowledge Meher Baba as the deepest inspiration for my life and work.

Contents

Foreword

BY LYNNE MCTAGGART

Author and spokesperson on consciousness, the new physics, and the practices of conventional and alternative medicine.

It's becoming increasingly clear that we have outgrown the rules we live by. The fractures in our global economic model – with the increasing divide between rich and poor, the worldwide threats posed by terrorism and major political upheaval, and the twin crises of global warming and exhaustion of the earth's natural resources – all suggest that something is fundamentally wrong with the way we have chosen to live our lives.

Many influences – including philosophy, religion, history – have helped to write our story, but our primary modern-day author is science, which fashions most of the big ideas we hold about the way the world works and our place within it. For more than 300 years, largely thanks to the discoveries of British scientists Isaac Newton and, later, Charles Darwin, our worldview has been fashioned by a story of separation and competitive individualism – of distinct and isolated entities competing for survival in a universe of limited resource.

With the catchphrase "survival of the fittest" Charles Darwin unleashed upon the world a metaphor that has come to represent the human experience: *life as war*. Competition and individual gain are the engines that drive the societies of most modern developed countries – the engines of our economy, even of our relationships. Any individual or population supposedly thrives only at another one's expense. This zero-sum metaphor, which is a *leitmotif* in all our lives, reflects the very same mindset that has created every one of the large global crises now threatening to destroy us.

That scientific story is now obsolete. We're on the brink of a revolution in science that challenges every one of our cherished beliefs about how the universe operates and how we define ourselves. An entirely new scientific story is emerging that has overturned many of our basic Newtonian and Darwinian assumptions, including the most basic premise of all: the sense of our world as a set of separate entities in competition for survival.

The latest evidence from quantum physics demonstrates that the universe is not a collection of individual, self-contained phenomena operating according to fixed laws in time and space, but a dynamic *relationship*, an irreducible whole, in which matter is now understood to exist in a vast quantum web of connection. Frontier biologists, psychologists and sociologists have all discovered that individuals are far less individual than we thought they were. As the latest evidence reveals, cooperation and partnership, not dominance, is fundamental to the biological makeup of all living things. In fact, nature's most fundamental drive is not competition, but wholeness.

These discoveries carry vast implications, not only about how we choose to define ourselves, but also about how we ought to live our lives. They suggest that most of us are living counter to our true nature. But applying these lessons in some practical way requires nothing less than making ourselves anew. They demand a drastic change in the way we relate to ourselves and all other living things, a new way of seeing, a new mindset that respects unity and connection over competition and separation. To achieve this, we need to adopt a new definition of what it means to be human. We need some new rules to live by.

James O'Dea has long been the passionate author of a new rulebook, first as former director of the Washington, DC, office of Amnesty International, and then as president and now on the extended faculty of the Institute of Noetic Sciences and co-director of the Social Healing Project. He is both visionary and peacemaker; consequently, his definition of peace extends beyond the simple cessation of fighting, or the victory of one side or another, for he recognizes that individual pain can contaminate entire societies. "We live", as he says in this book, "in a world of wound contagion." Divided societies represent not simply a war against individuals or ethnic groups but, as the German theologian Geiko Müller-Fahrenholz once put it, a "war of the world with itself".

James O'Dea's mission is to help individuals and groups recover their sense of unity by smoothing the way for warring sides to reconcile and forgive. For a decade he and Dr Judith Thompson co-hosted "compassion and social healing" dialogues, which invited frank confrontation between members of highly divided social and political groups – Republican and loyalist Northern Irish, Turkish and Greek Cypriots, Israelis and Palestinians – in an attempt to heal shared wounds.

During those dialogues James guided participants in ways to move the emphasis away from who is right and who is wrong, and toward who is wounded and how to heal. He discovered certain processes of deep listening and dialogue to be the most powerful of healers – far more than punishment or even restitution. Their effectiveness comes from dismantling both perpetrator and victim, allowing each to acknowledge the deep truth of an experience and his or her bond in that history. Central to this process was the opportunity for deep understanding of both pain and shame, which ultimately proved the catalyst for liberating people from hurt and guilt. Both sides were encouraged to see themselves as part of a greater whole, and their disagreement as something akin to an interrupted connection.

In *Soul Awakening Practice* James has an even more ambitious agenda: to establish a new consciousness of unity and connection. This book is an unapologetic instruction manual, framed in a series of meditations and prayers, for a new evolutionary consciousness. Each piece has been carefully constructed, because James understands that thoughts – whether expressed through prayer or through intention – are the most powerful of change-makers. Thanks to the new science we now have evidence that thoughts have the extraordinary capacity to change physical matter. Through centuries of tradition, we know that prayers are the most persuasive and totemic words of all: they reach deep into the soul, carrying with them the mysterious capacity to catalyse individual and collective transformation.

To fuel his own meditations James calls upon an eclectic mix of thought leaders representing a variety of traditions, ranging from futurists such as Barbara Marx Hubbard and Ervin László, to experts on transpersonal psychology and meditation such as Anodea Judith and Michael A Singer, to Sufi Muslim Kabir Helminski and Hopi Native American Mona Polacca. Each offers original ways to open the heart, dissolve wounds and allow love to flow. The resulting compilation of all these synergistic voices offers a detailed roadmap to a new world.

This book is meant to be savoured slowly. Like a modern-day Rumi, James O'Dea offers heartachingly beautiful exhortations on every page, each an invitation to a radical new way of thinking and being. "You listen to insult and argument. Why not listen for peace?" he writes. "If you have difficulty seeing past condemnation of perpetrators, focus your attention on their hidden wounds." He reminds us constantly of the unity our common humanity yearns for: "peace is not the absence of war," he argues. "It is the pervasive presence of compassionate connection."

Do not mistake this book for an easy read. *Soul Awakening Practice* is meant to be a call to a new type of arms, offering a path for spiritual seekers of every persuasion. James is unapologetic in his aim of shaping a new type of Darwinism, which honours the survival of the most loving, "leading us through natural selection processes to create an advantage for compassionate and collaborative human beings". This is a book that demands active engagement and daily practice – indeed a revolution in your everyday living.

As *Soul Awakening Practice* powerfully argues, spiritual engagement is today's moral imperative. Faced with some of the greatest upheavals and challenges in the entire history of humanity, we are one of the most important generations that have ever lived. Each of the major choices we make today will affect our children's children – and indeed the world for all time.

At this period of great upheaval, *Soul Awakening Practice* offers a profound message of hope. "Cycles [of wounding]", writes James, "can be skilfully interrupted when there is a commitment to the kind of truth that allows people to express their deepest pain and dream a new story together."

May this book be the catalyst for you to dream big.

Lynne McTaggart

Introduction

This book is about contemplation and action. It's about the conjunction between the inner quest for revelation and the equally significant quest for the coherent embodiment of that revelation in the outer sphere of our personal and collective journeys.

At one level *Soul Awakening Practice* is a manual of spiritual instruction, shedding light and guidance for personal transformation. But it's also about bringing the soul's light and wisdom into a world aching for deep social transformation. It offers the seeker a rich structure of practice combining prayer/mantra with passionate insight and inspiration for tangible ways for us to become spiritual warriors in the world ... or better still, spiritual peacemakers.

Before explaining how to use this book, I should like to provide some background thoughts about prayer in general.

Prayer has many subtly different faces and dimensions, but it's often associated with supplication. We pray *for* someone or something. We pray when we have urgent needs. We pray when crisis strikes, or when we feel lost or persecuted. Prayer becomes a helpline to God when we're desperate.

Prayer is also a way of expressing gratitude – for loving relationships, for health, for success, for resources, for good fortune, for the end of a period of trials, and for prayers answered.

There's also a great tradition of prayer as a channel for praising and affirming God's qualities and the magnificence of divine love, mercy and justice. Such prayers often serve to reinforce a particular theology or system of faith.

"Ask and you shall receive" is still a mainstream concept in the popular imagination, but *how* we ask has been undergoing a sea change. The New Thought movement added a dimension to supplicatory prayer that removes any anxious neediness in the person praying, replacing a sense of inadequacy – of a lack that needs to be rectified – with a positive affirmation. Gratitude and praise are integrated into a new state of consciousness whereby all needs are resolved. One enters into gratitude and praise as a means to fully align with divine will and celebrate its perfection. Consciousness then energetically shifts toward solutions, instead of being caught in a whirlpool of unmet needs. This approach places more attention on one's state of being when praying. In the process it brings prayer closer to meditative states, where the goal is to gain insight.

New Thought and the Positive Psychology movement have reinforced each other. Positive Psychology urges us to spend less time in problem analysis and more time in giving energy to solutions. At the same time, contemporary neuroscience has affirmed our capacity to create new neural pathways as we commit to new ways of thinking and to lifestyle changes. Rather than being caught in states of disempowerment, where we find ourselves pleading for help, we can pray in such a way that our imaginative engagement in desired outcomes helps to rewire our brains.

These developments also synchronize with insights emerging from consciousness research, which has revealed the pivotal role of attitudes, beliefs and worldviews in governing behaviour. We may find ourselves praying in terms of one set of assumptions but actually believing, deep down, in something quite different. Our conditioning runs deep into the unconscious, where old, unexamined beliefs trigger or control our responses. As we become conscious of embedded beliefs, deriving from our personal or cultural history, we can transform them to match changes that have taken place in our own experience or in the world at large. Our whole worldview can then shift to bring about a new understanding of ourselves and of the nature of reality.

We can no longer separate prayer from what we've learned from contemporary mind–body science, with its improved understanding of attention and its effect on *in*tention. Intention acts as the guidance system for where you put your attention: without clear intention your mind wanders all over the place. The boundaries of what we think of as prayer are expanding. Groundbreaking work has been done by Lynne McTaggart, integrating scientific and spiritual insight in exploring the remarkable potential of collective intention-setting.

We also know now that bringing the heart into *coherence* with conscious deep breathing accompanied by feelings of love and gratefulness positively changes the biochemistry of the blood, brings a calming resonance to the brain and promotes an overall sense of well-being. It isn't surprising that the heart plays a leading role in prayer, but our understanding of this full synchronization of the mind–body system is relatively new.

Of course, the ancients, as well as mystics from the great spiritual traditions, understood, experienced and practised this deep harmonization of heart–mind–body. In the East, in addition to a complex array of advanced meditation and yogic disciplines in Hinduism and Buddhism, the *mantra* has been a key practice in creating a deep, resonant and focused awareness. By a repetition of sacred sounds, chants or short phrases, the seeker's attention is concentrated on a divine theme. Sometimes the mantra is accompanied by a visualization. The alchemy of breath, sound, vibration and meaning creates a whole mind–body experience.

Through this alchemy the consciousness of the seeker gains access to higher states of compassion, kindness and subtlety, as well as exposure to profound truth.

In the West, Sufism has its own kind of mantra practice, called *Dhikr*. Dhikr is essentially the remembrance of God and the affirmation of God's qualities through repetition of sacred phrases and of the names of God. Exponents greatly emphasize placing awareness in the centre of the heart. As with other forms of prayerful and contemplative practice, Dhikr is a way to cultivate an ongoing experience of higher reality as we go about our daily lives. Famously, Dhikr can be expressed through movement and sacred dance.

Judaism also has its rich traditions of expressing the sacred through sound, while in Native American and other shamanic cultures the same function is performed by chants and the beating of drums. Such mantric practice can lead to extraordinary states of consciousness, subtle energy experiences, radical insight and an ecstatic sense of awe and reverence.

In Christian mysticism there's a distinction between the various forms of internally and externally vocalized prayer and the cultivation of an intimate experience of divine presence. What's known in Christianity as *contemplative prayer* is a constant cultivation of relationship with God: contemplative prayer is, in essence, any method that leads to a continuous experience of divine being. There's an emphasis on being fed and nourished by a loving God whose presence is felt in every dimension of one's life. Contemplatives know that all noise and bustle are tiny ripples across a pervasive silence behind the visible universe – the place in which, they say, the voice of

God can be heard. Like prayers of the heart (whether inwardly or outwardly recited), contemplative prayer is about quieting the mind and allowing one's being to be saturated with God's presence, which fills one with love, insight and guidance.

We shouldn't be overly concerned about whether or not words are employed – what's critical is the amplification of one's core being. A growing number of people have taken up Eastern meditation practices to cultivate a calm, centered awareness, a state of loving kindness or union with the guru, and in these a mantra may or may not be employed. In Western spirituality, meditation is practised in the sense of meditating *upon* something, such as an aspect or quality of the divine. In Buddhism one empties the mind. The "prayer of the heart" as taught by Brother Lawrence employs words, whereas Buddhist Vipassana practice on the nature of reality is evoked in silent breath work. But whatever the means, the seeker's goal is to gain intimate guidance and insight.

All these forms of mystical prayer and meditation combine two complementary tendencies. One of these is *giving* heart-centered attention; the other is *receiving* a connection with a higher reality – whether described as immersion in the Presence, the touch of the Beloved, the gift of Illumination, Perfect Insight or the taste of Oneness. Even though, in some cases, the mystic experience takes place within a specially designated ceremonial space, the goal is not a ritualized exchange but rather an intense communion that can be passionate and soul-baring.

It's in this spirit of both giving and receiving that the Soul Awakening Prayer came to me. I think of this prayer as one of *communing*. When we commune, there's an intimacy of connection that evokes subtle states of consciousness. Freed from the linear grammar of language, we gravitate toward deep conjunction.

Communion creates an environment where boundaries dissolve and the mind is suffused with resonances that speak to the whole of our being. As in the world of dreams, we enter into a new language of multiple, archetypal meanings. You might say that this is similar to the way in which quantum reality opens up a universe that defies the rules of mechanical physics. Once liberated from linear logic, we can experience tidal shifts in consciousness directly and gain precious insight.

In what I am calling a "prayer of communing", rather than being anchors, *words* become sails that catch the winds of subtle transmission and carry us into the territory of spiritual encounter and revelation. These words can be very simple, but nonetheless highly effective in transporting us from the ego-dominated, endlessly "chattering" mind to a quiet, selfless place of intimate connection with higher reality. People who have worked with the simple Soul Awakening Prayer, as presented in the pages that follow, report experiencing a cascading flow of transmission as they move from one line of affirmation to the next.

Prayers of communing that are a true gift from higher reality emanate from what mystics refer to as the Sacred Mystery. They are instruments of transmission from the higher source. They are deeply coherent and revelatory. While such prayers can evoke personal intimacy and speak directly to the heart, they also reveal impersonal principles of abiding truth, calling upon us to silence the pleas of the ego and instead give our service to a suffering world with whatever skills we have at our disposal.

My point about "coherence" requires emphasis, since the tendencies of our age turn more towards *in*coherence. In modern times in the West belief is often presented as a shopping list of choices. We navigate imperfectly among the options, picking from a smorgasbord of faiths, principles, opinions and half-digested "facts" without any clear sense of what's right and what's true. Sadly, our view of the spirit – of all that's of prime importance in our lives – can become random and incoherent. This is why, in addition to the simple Soul Awakening Prayer, there's an abundance of contemplative reflections in this book, aimed at activating coherent personal and collective transformation.

As an antidote to all this chaos, the *Soul Awakening Practice* offers a deeply coherent worldview – a map that integrates ancient wisdom with modern science and psychology. It invites you to integrate contemplation and action in your daily spiritual practice.

In accord with these principles I've invited guest perspectives from distinguished individuals in science, cosmology, evolutionary theory, yoga, Sufism and indigenous wisdom to contribute precious insights to this book. Their various contributions, I believe, harmonize perfectly with the prayer itself, with my own contemplative reflections, and with the 15 key spiritual concepts I've outlined in the final section of the book to create a deep coherence.

My own contemplative reflections integrate all the separate but complementary elements within a format that allows the reader to slow down and to digest the ideas in a prayerful way. This is a new prayer book for modern times.

It's a prayer book of contemplation and practice for evolutionaries and activists, for deep ecologists, for spiritual seekers engaged in passionate renewal and for all those thirsty for a spiritually coherent worldview. In this crucible of intense and rapid change that we're experiencing together, I hope that you'll find in these pages the inspiration and guidance needed for personal and planetary soul awakening. More than anything we need to embody our prayers and meditation in transformational practices that recreate our world in the image of our soul's true wisdom.

May the prayers of a transforming global humanity communing together lead us home to peace radiating in all beings, throughout nature and in all systems of governance, commerce and community.

The Soul Awakening Prayer

Soul Awakening

Heart Opening

Light Shining

Love Flowing

Wounds Dissolving

Peace Radiating

How to Work with the Soul Awakening Practice

THE SOUL AWAKENING PRAYER

The Soul Awakening Prayer has just six lines, given in full on page 13. These lines are intended to be voiced once, phrase by phrase, in the order given. The whole prayer is then repeated four times. With repetition as a whole, the prayer reveals a spiritual universe of both power and beauty.

Allow yourself to enter a peaceful state for communing with the higher Self, then speak aloud each phrase of the prayer once or sound it in your heart's core. It's good to direct your intention in repeating the prayer to move from a personal focus to a collective one. That is to say, as you repeat the whole prayer, voicing it four times as I've mentioned, you move from personal to planetary intention, as described below:

First
As you say or resonate each line of the prayer in your heart, visualize your own soul awakening, your heart opening, the light shining in your heart and mind, love flowing through you, all your wounds dissolving and peace radiating from the core of your being.

Second

Focus on someone you wish to commune with – a child, loved one or friend, or someone you wish to direct a special intention towards. You can visualize soul awakening, heart opening, light shining, love flowing, wounds dissolving and peace radiating together with them. You can also focus this second step with those physically practising the prayer with you – your soul mate or prayer group.

Third

Now visualize the soul awakening process expanding to include and touch everyone you're connected to – family, friends and colleagues. Feel the energy of the prayer rippling out and resonating throughout the field of all your connections.

Fourth

The set of four rounds of the prayer ends with a visualization of planetary soul awakening, of collective heart opening, of light shining in the heart of all human beings, of love flowing throughout humanity, of all our wounds being dissolved and peace radiating throughout the Earth.

*

The Soul Awakening Prayer is to be practised daily by individuals, couples and small affinity and prayer groups. It has also been used to open board meetings, spiritual retreats and conferences.

THE CONTEMPLATIVE REFLECTIONS, ESSAYS AND 15 KEY SPIRITUAL CONCEPTS

The contemplative reflections on each phrase of the prayer are designed to help to deepen your own subtle practice of communing with higher reality and to touch your imagination in ways that spark awakening, insight and action. Read them slowly and thoughtfully at any time, absorbing them deep into the fabric of your mind. Take a deep breath before turning each page. Let the thoughts expressed become second nature to you.

Treat the short guest essays as an additional way to deepen your practice by exposing you to relevant wisdom. If you don't understand any of the points made, let them enter your mind anyway: trust their authentic and soulful insights.

The 15 key spiritual concepts at the end of the book will hopefully help to reinforce important underlying ideas.

*

Let the light in your heart guide your way.

CONTEMPLATIVE REFLECTIONS ON

Soul Awakening

The soul's awakening is one of the most dramatic events in the entire universe. It is filled with immeasurable significance.

Until the moment your soul begins to awaken,

it has been like a seed not yet fully opened. The

sheath of your soul – its husk – is your mind with

its vast array of impressions slowly evolving

through direct experience. The kernel of the seed

waiting to sprout is your eternal self.

You have been on a very long journey through lifetimes of dramatically diverse and arduous experiences. Every significant experience is part of a continuum of connected lifetimes acting as a record of your progress towards eventual soul awakening.

All of these testing experiences shake the husk encasing your soul – nudging it inexorably toward its final cracking open and awakening to its sacred destiny.

_____

Your soul has been on a journey even longer than lifetimes. It first travels through Nature's evolutionary journey before waking to human consciousness. Thus every human being is born as a hologram of the wholeness of creation and as a fulfilment of the spiritual goal of evolution.

_____

_____

Before it fully awakens, the soul is a hidden witness to the entire evolutionary process. As our DNA so brilliantly reveals, human life and all life on planet Earth are inextricably woven together as part of one truly momentous evolving story.

_____

The joy of the dolphin, the caterpillar's ingenious transformation, the majesty of the jaguar and the soaring freedom of the eagle are imprinted in the collective field of consciousness as life's prodigious experiments in learning. Celebrate this lineage of creative emergence in Nature that you are an integral part of!

From the inner core of evolution the soul begins its awakening into the field of human consciousness, with its vast potential, where it will finally reveal to you your most sacred origins and your ultimate destiny to return to your Source.

_____

Your soul must first experience the fierce intensity of living through much testing over many lifetimes in dramatically contrasting life circumstances before it can fully awaken. Then, the awakening finally happens in the form of a powerful and spiritually charged breakthrough lifetime.

_____

When you are ready to see through the illusory nature of all that divides humanity and when you are drawn to passionately serve the evolving story of the unity of all beings, your soul is empowered to shine its ecstatic, all-knowing light into your heart. You experience the birth of higher, soul-guided intuition.

Soul finally begins to suffuse your consciousness as the eternal torchbearer of universal love and as the luminous wisdom of the one Source of all life. You feel radiated with a fire that calls you to be ever more profoundly true to your higher self as it emerges with fresh responsibility into a deeply challenged world.

Soul calls you out of hiding. It takes you to the edge. Then it nudges you over the edge. It knows you must fly or live with your quest for meaning unfulfilled. A false sense of security is always the first thing to go. There can be no hedging when you take the high dive from illusion to reality.

_____

A moment of such cosmic significance as the awakening of your soul sheds light on the nature and purpose of creation and why we are here on Earth. Secrets of divinity are shared. Now you can leave the confines of the suffocating limitations that have stifled your life force.

_____

_____

Soul spins the scattered clay of your life into a living chalice fired in the furnace of an almost unbearable beauty and grace. You are spirit made manifest in a world crawling out of the ooze of its own chaos, creative exuberance and suffering.

_____

Soul's unique task is to draw human conscious-ness inwards and upwards on the great journey back to the one Source. Your turbulent mind's cacophony and confusion now dissolve in the face of penetrating clarity and higher insight into the infinite, eternal, undivided reality.

_____

As your soul awakens, it begins to permeate your psyche with wholeness, your heart with love's subtle harmony and your mind with visionary insight and a vibrant moral conscience. You are on your way to becoming a new creation. But the world will still manufacture its own meanness, crudity and calculated self-interest to try to subvert your progress, so that it can bind you to the false security of the status quo.

_____

Soul's awakening journey is one that inevitably moves beyond seemingly relentless suffering to a state of profound celebration. Once we experience the celebration of our true soulful nature, we dance with ceaseless passion for the new life and the new forms of healing, peace and justice.

Intellect can envision and explore new worlds, but it is awakened soul that synchronizes body, heart, mind and spirit. Soul brings universal truth into visionary embodiment and manifests as evolutionary creativity in action.

Mind gets lost in fantasies, whereas Soul feeds pure imagination, which contains all the codes needed for us to manifest planetary healing and deep social renewal. Perfection emerges out of pure imagination and the awakened courage to embody Soul's beckoning. Evolution's great game is to lift each of us up to play creatively in God's imagination.

_____

Soul's essence is so united with Source that it reveals itself to be nothing less than God seeded within us. God remains hidden in our souls until we hear the call to perfect unity, commit to selfless service and can dare to live into the truly awakened states of divine audacity.

_____

_____

Soul's awakening not only heralds a deep change of heart in your life, it is also the glorious entrance to the grace of the spiritual path and to the rigorous requirements of returning to your divine home while simultaneously manifesting the expression of universal love in action here on Earth.

_____

As your soul awakens, you are given your true spiritual work. Your whole being begins to shift its axis to revolve around being an authentic and fearless ambassador of universal truth and unconditional love. You will be asked to shred any remaining boundaries of narrow self-interest. True heroism is necessary to live a spiritual life, since such a life inevitably challenges the sanctimonious righteousness of religious and social conformity.

Soul can never be a part of religious claims to superiority: it emanates from a reality that respects all explorations of Truth and ignites transcendent spiritual principles which then become actualized as incarnate expressions of Love and Mercy.

Soul awakening is the summoning of your own essence to take you home to infinite being. This is the long-awaited lifetime in which you will never again turn away from the path.

—————————————————

Contemplate the long and arduous journey that has taken you to this moment and be grateful for it all. Yes, grateful, for all the lifetimes that brought you through the chaos, turmoil and ecstasy of your own becoming.

—————————————————

Now the acquisitive mind that has brought you to this place must itself be dissolved. All your baggage must go. A good spiritual practice will help you clear your subconscious mind where most of your really debilitating patterns are packed away.

All that you have clung to along the way must now be courageously released in surrender to the divine plan for creation. Soul awakens when you are no longer clinging to narrow personal achievement and the petty ego's need for recognition. Contemplate your own unsurpassed greatness existing without ego.

Your hands are empty and your arms stretched wide as you embrace the truth of your soul's deepest identity and its creative assignment in manifesting evolved consciousness. You are a speck becoming a cosmos: stay open. What will unfold will blow your mind: this is not a ride for the tightfisted.

_____

Beyond personal memory you remember who you

are as pure lucid spirit.

_____

In soul awakening the core of your being consciously reconnects with the heart of the universe. Intimate communion with a cosmos that manifests through and beyond the physical becomes your inner compass for the journey home. You are free at last to live the greater story and explore the depths of your own wild and beautiful self as it voyages into the deep space of reality.

Soul's awakening stirs reverence in the heart for all life and a deep desire to serve and protect all beings. Soul awakening dissolves separation. It is a remembrance of whole life, whole system reality. Thus, soul awakening brings with it more integrated holistic solutions.

Soul calls us to live passionately and fearlessly and to own our shadow. Soul knows that trapped energy is still a form of energy and that this energy can be liberated. We call trapped energy by names such as guilt, shame, frustration and so on, but they are all just energies waiting to be freed from dense states of consciousness to become more subtle and refined.

Soul knows that, even though the process may take eons, all beings will eventually be liberated from the energies of destructive greed and violent conflict. This knowledge is the mother of soulful and conscious activism.

_____

Allow a deep sense of awe to fill your awareness

as you perceive the gravity and beauty of your

soul's awakening.

_____

———————————————

Remember your soul is a hologram of your true identity and purpose as a being both universal and local. Your local address on planet Earth is not by any stretch your final destination. But it is your passport to the cosmos.

———————————————

Soul's awakening lights a fire of irreversible transformation whose story ends only in our collective experience of enlightenment and peace. Each soul helps to liberate other souls when it awakens. Just think how many souls will awaken because you started to live from your essence.

Out of the dark mud, the lotus catches fire in light and beauty. Yours is the mud and yours the lotus, on this epic journey to soul awakening. So too for all. A great soul-driven planetary civilization will rise out of the dark but potent struggle of evolving humanity, allowing us to thrive at last in the light of peace, the full spectrum of beauty in diversity and the restoration of profound harmony with Nature.

Soul Awakening

BY BARBARA MARX HUBBARD

Author of seven books on social and planetary evolution, and a documentary film maker, Barbara Marx Hubbard is co-founder of the World Future Society, the Association for Global New Thought and the Foundation for Conscious Evolution.

In the Evolutionary Age, soul awakening becomes the conscious expression of the process of creation uniquely embodied in each of us.

Our 'vocation of destiny' is the impulse of evolution emerging as our passion to *be* more, *love* more, *create* more.

This passion to create expresses the genius of evolution animating the very essence of our being. The soul awakening is God's way of evolving humans now. It is God becoming human so that humans can become like God.

The fulfilment of the soul awakening is our union with the God within. The impulse and the individual become One.

A new human is evolving as the impulse of creation incarnates as us. We become guided from within by the sheer magnitude of the purpose of evolution as it influences one's own yearning. Our vocation of destiny is the impulse of the creative process focused as our unique passion to evolve.

The soul awakening animates the person to become co-creator with the Divine.

In this first Age of *Conscious* Evolution in which we live, Soul is intensifying its expression. We are "Generation One". There are no elders. No one on Earth has been through a set of global crises and opportunities on this scale. Our generation is facing the interruption of life on Earth caused in part by our own actions.

As the first generation entering this evolutionary crisis and opportunity, we are animated, charged, excited to express our soul's awakening in a new and vital way.

Many systems on Earth are failing. Yet at the same time alternative systems are evolving through innovators, co-creators, lovers of life. Each of us is called to leadership in the co-creation of an emerging healthy world.

By saying yes to our vocation of destiny we become ever more animated by the process of creation. New humans are being born within those whose souls are awakening now at this particular time of transformation on planet Earth.

We are all members of a planetary body. The whole planetary organism is evolving in the great multi-billion-year tradition of evolution.

Each of us is awakening as a member of this planetary body, integrating into a new whole system whether we like each other or not. Our communication systems are linking into a vast global network, our environment is completely interconnected, our defence systems are pointed at one another with thermonuclear weapons that can destroy all life on Earth.

At the same time our new capacities, especially in high technology – nanotechnology, biotechnologies, quantum computing, robotics, artificial intelligence and far more – are giving us the powers of gods. We are becoming a new species: *Homo universalis*. Through our high-tech genius we can restore the Earth, free ourselves from hunger, disease and war, and explore the farther reaches of inner space and the cosmos beyond our mother Earth.

Our crisis is the birth of a universal species. We are the first generation born during this "birth".

The soul awakening in this generation is entering a new phase of connection, with everyone called to play their part. The soul is expressing not only the mystical bliss of oneness with the All. It is alive in us also as the passionate desire to create, to realize our unique potential in specific functions needed during this crisis of birth.

Everyone is needed. Everyone is called.

What is our experience of Soul at this stage of planetary birth? It expresses ever more clearly its passion. Evolution is yearning for more intimacy, more love.

We all have a memory of the past as well as the future encoded in every cell.

In our mother's womb we have experienced the whole evolutionary story – starting with our life as a single cell, then through multi-cellular teamwork, a fish, a mammal, an early human and then a new-born human, coded with the potential for conscious growth in the evolutionary process.

So now, at the stage of the planetary birth, our soul is awakening us to a new level of awareness, a new memory of the story of creation.

Now is when we begin to remember our 13.7-billion-year "birth narrative". The atoms, molecules, cells, organs and brain of our being were created in the mysterious cauldron of evolution. We are coded to remember the past and also the future.

The soul awakening in the period of transition to our birth as a fully awakened species reveals to us that consciousness is omnipresent. The pre-transition mystical experience is of boundlessness and no Self; the evolutionary post-transition experience is universal personhood, whose self is unique, universal, formless and not bound by ego: rather, it is a consciously manifested expression of Source or Spirit animating each of us.

The soul awakening enlivens a greater dimension of our being. We collectively begin to experience our Universal

Self, free of the field of Earth, on the other side of the long transition from *Homo sapiens sapiens* to *Homo universalis*: ecstatic, a radiant flash of joy – like the sun breaking through the clouds.

We finally come to realize that we are all omnipresent consciousness manifesting in a physical body, like the universe of which we are a part. We all have continuity of consciousness with the Consciousness that is creating us.

Remembering the story of our cosmic birth is vital to the full-scale recognition, cultivation and incarnation of soul awakening. Our soul is aware of the whole story of creation and transmits that awareness to us.

When our soul awakens, each of us is guided to take our part within cosmogenesis. We are the *universe in person*. This is the primary purpose of every incarnation now.

During our planetary birthing process, a new form of spirituality is emerging. It is an evolutionary spirituality – the spirituality of incarnation. Jesus said: "If you have seen me, you have seen the Father." We can now say: "If you have seen me, you have seen the whole process of creation, the soul awakening in me as me." We and the Source are one. Religion itself is now evolving.

I encapsulate the essence of soul awakening as an expression of what I call the "4 Es" of conscious evolution:

THE FIRST E IS ETERNITY

We are one with Source. The source of creation is alive in every one of us. The ever-recurring Big Bang is exploding within us as we are animated by the whole story of creation. Mother/Father God becomes the Godhead evolving within us, God yearning for more life.

We are evolution becoming self-aware. We are animated by God's longing to develop co-creators with the Divine, in the image of God, in the image of Source, Spirit, Consciousness … there is as yet no good evolutionary word for God evolving continually through us as us.

THE SECOND E IS EMBODY

We are a résumé of the whole story of creation. In every cell of our being is encoded the memory not only of the miracle of the self-organizing person in our mother's womb, but also of the awareness that we are growing seeds of the astounding story of our emergence from no thing at all to everything that was, is and will be evolving.

This is the moment of our planetary birth. We are each encoded with the dawning awareness of our unique function in the new phase of planetary evolution. Like the imaginal cells in the body of the caterpillar, we are coded with the unique importance of our greater function within the planetary body. We are seeking to know where we fit best in the evolving system.

The soul is awakening to the realization that we each have a unique cosmic mission. Everyone is called to their posts. The hour of our birth is at hand.

THE THIRD E IS EMERGE

Each of us stands at the growing edge of evolution. We are moving forward towards radical newness, like a baby being born from the womb to the world. Whatever work we have done, more is coming. When we say "Yes" to the impulse of creation within us, we become newer every day. We are "thresholding" – that is, crossing the threshold from one phase of human evolution to the next.

When we say "Yes" to our emerging potential, our cells receive the message: *There is more for you to do*. They begin to regenerate.

When the soul awakens within us, the "genius of evolution", the "supra-mental" creativity of universal life, flows through us activating the awakening human. We know more, become more, give more, love more. Our new functions emerge. Our life purpose expands.

When we say a full "Yes" from the source of our being, we find ourselves informed by the genius of evolution ever more directly.

We are becoming a new archetype on Earth, embodying the process of creation as our own expression of creativity and love.

THE FOURTH E IS EROS

Evolution is the expression of love. Love evolves through attraction, quark with quark, particle with particle, cell with cell, human with human, tribe with tribe, culture with culture.

As our soul awakens we are attracted to one another across all barriers of race, class, colour, gender and creed. The awakening of evolutionary love within us becomes the strange attracting force, as powerful as sexuality. This is the evolution of sexuality.

We are attracted to join, not our genes to have a baby, but our genius to give birth to our greater self and to our more creative work in the world. Massive pro-creation transforms into a new phase of collective co-creation.

Joining genius is nature's way to evolve the world. The attraction we feel towards another whose genius more fully animates our own is an expression of the evolution of sexuality toward supra-sexuality. It brings joy, love, newness. It is self-rewarding. We become "telerotic" – filled with high purpose and connective love. We experience "vocational arousal", the passion to co-create.

Sexuality becomes sacred when it's expressed through joining the genius to create with a shared purpose for the world. The sacredness of sex to have a child, to reproduce the species, becomes the sacredness of sex to evolve ourselves and the world. The union for shared purpose gives birth to a greater world through joining in love. The divine plan is that the world will be evolved through love, not fear.

Soul awakening is arising in many of us. We are attracted to the future as an organism progressing toward the unknown. We are co-founding a new evolutionary family of humanity, arising in every culture. We are being connected with each other and with the Source through our rapidly growing new planetary nervous system. We are preparing the way for a planetary awakening through a unique self symphony in which every one of us expresses our unique note of creativity.

The symphony is orchestrated by an omnicentric, self-organizing universe in the great multi-billion-year tradition of the rise of consciousness, freedom and synergistic order.

At the very peak of the planetary awakening the soul awakening expresses itself through enough of us simultaneously to shift the consciousness field of Earth from fear to love.

We open our collective eyes and see that we are good, we are whole, we are born to universal life, on this Earth and beyond. In the field of resonance and love, the lights from universal existence come toward us. We smile our first planetary smile.

CONTEMPLATIVE REFLECTIONS ON

Heart Opening

The heart is a window to the awakening soul.

In fact, it is the only means of experiencing

this cosmic event unfolding within your being.

But you must learn many exquisitely difficult

spiritual lessons on how to open your heart wide

enough for the light of your soul to fully enter in.

When the heart opens, it senses an unfolding connection to a wide universe pulsing with unbounded compassion and love far beyond our preoccupation with narrow personal needs and desires. The heart, seeing for the first time the community of all souls, is indelibly imprinted with reverence for every soul's journey out into space and time and back to its timeless home in the divine source.

When the personal heart is introduced to the spaciousness of the universal heart, it beholds the stunning vista of the path that lies before it and experiences the first in what will become a series of radical transformations. Inside the expanding heart we keep shedding all our temporary personas until we reach the soul's eternal identity.

_____

Cultivating spaciousness encourages limitless communion between the opening heart and the awakening soul. A living conscious cosmos opens inside you. You become expansive and filled with intimate connection to Life.

_____

_____

Without space and silence the heart remains

tight and self-concerned.

_____

―――――――――――――――――――――

Spiritual inspiration arises when the heart is given the freedom to fly toward the soul's divinely planned unfolding. In the fiery light of awakening and opening, true worship and obedience rise out of the heart's core. Only through this freely offered obedience will you muster the courage to incarnate a heart-sourced, soul-directed life.

―――――――――――――――――――――

When the heart begins to release selfish preoccupations, it is drawn into the sphere of the eternal Beloved, which is the only power in the universe capable of uniting you with the molten sun of your own soul's essence. The self meets Self.

Once the spacious love of the universal heart is glimpsed, the personal heart experiences a realization of its own state of entanglement, constriction, clutter, attachment and make-believe. Now, at last, you find true perspective. There is a deeply precious sense that you can now step out of ego confinement.

Wide sunlit orchards of love, forgiveness and tenderness are revealed when the heart opens, but not far off we find that unresolved hurts still exist in the shadows, as well as possibly more painful feelings that confine the heart's powerful subtle energy field.

_____

The heart's opening slowly defies the gravitational pull of buried wounds. Faith is now alive and vividly experienced, not just a set of ideas you have been told to believe. It has the power to lift you out of the ashes of crisis and despair, and can even enable you to soar towards complete liberation. Heart opening propels you into new life like no other force.

_____

As the heart opens, it is drawn to pure freedom. It replaces constant nitpicky control and management of feelings with spontaneous originality and profound inquiry, with love and devotion. Once you begin to live in freedom, you will find yourself moving towards an even deeper form of spiritual abandonment.

It is one of the lessons of lifetimes that the heart has the power to experience great extremes of emotion without imprisoning them in the unconscious as unhealthy attachments or unresolved wounds. As we evolve, we expand our emotional range: when the heart opens, we do not suppress our emotions, we orchestrate them over many more octaves of feeling.

There are many things that can keep the heart shuttered. Our work is to purify our inner field of emotional and mental awareness in order to clean out oppressive and stagnant energies, preventing them from blocking the heart's pristine light and restricting its natural state of freedom. Begin this work by loving yourself, because loving yourself opens the door to your true self.

———————————————

Without the heart's ability to transcend separation and division, the world would not be anywhere we could live. The heart is a healer, because when it is open it listens so deeply that it dissolves barriers of fear and resentment.

———————————————

The heart is a phoenix capable of rising out of the ashes of hatred, war and terror.

_____

Your heart has the power to share the substance of unconditional love with everyone, despite hostility, insult and rejection. Devoid of narcissism, it is an agent of both personal and social transformation. Great leadership inspires heart opening by dissolving meanness and exuding a generous spirit.

_____

_____

When it opens, your heart feels subtle currents of grace that lift you and prompt you to soar towards the mystery of your destiny. You feel invited and welcomed as a part of a wider, totally inclusive universe. You are part of the whole breathtaking design of creation.

_____

Heart opening is a conscious act of participation in healing the self and others. It is an act of creative engagement with the spiritual ascension of humanity.

The masters of spiritual wisdom tell us that the heart is a mirror of the infinite and that we must polish it with constant attention. In a state of clear awareness, the heart sees beyond the limitations of time and space and touches the utter vastness of divine love.

Watch how the heart reaches stillness before it is drawn up toward the energy of the Beloved. In the space between breaths there is a love affair where heart and soul merge. In quantum reality every subatomic particle is pulsed, the whole universe creates breathing space for freshness and renewal.

_____

Science confirms the practice of building deep heart coherence through love and gratitude. When we feel compassion, the body's electrical and biochemical systems radiate peace and wellness.

_____

_____

Breathe into your heart so that it opens and

empties. Do not try to keep it full all the time. Let

it empty. Let it fill. You will discover as you do so

that you do not have to invent love or gratitude,

because they are natural forces in a universe

that could not exist without them.

_____

_____

Be advised: when the heart opens, it becomes a

different kind of warrior for truth and justice. It

does not confuse non-judgement and compassion

with moral neutrality.

_____

_____

In each breath let your heart open until it is spacious, wild and free. Only then will you flower in the field of God's limitless beauty and grace. Our teachers remind us that as we open up we will meet fires of resistance, but this is part of the purification process until the breath carries us into the garden in the centre of the heart – known to mystics as the garden within the flames.

_____

Heart Opening

BY ANODEA JUDITH

Author of many bestselling books on spirituality, psychology and social change, including groundbreaking works on the chakras, Anodea Judith is also renowned as a dynamic speaker and workshop leader, and as founder of Sacred Centers.

I've heard it said that the longest journey a person may take in their lifetime is the 18 inches from their head to their heart. This journey is more than a personal quest – it is a voyage from the inner temple of our own heart opening up to a larger matrix that connects us all globally. A global heart recognizes our commonality as sacred beings working together for a world that works, a planetary maturity that allows us to evolve together, as elements of a still larger matrix of universal love. Travelling from the personal heart to the global heart, and opening still further to an understanding of the heart of the wider universe, is the journey of our time.

Every day we are surrounded by miracles that demonstrate love. At the darkest time of the year, the pure white of snow reflects light, and is then stored on mountaintops to feed our streams in spring and summer. Leaves fall to the ground in autumn to compost and nourish new life in spring. Trees produce oxygen for us to breathe while absorbing our carbon dioxide – especially critical in these times of global warming. Nature abounds with love affairs, a daily demonstration to teach us how to connect.

Even the fact that you are reading these words is testament to a brain that can assemble dots of ink printed on a page into words that have meaning and, hopefully, convey deep truths about the reality where we have our being. That this book exists is testament to many unseen hands harvesting wood and making paper, printing and binding it into a book, and transporting its jewels to your heart. Whenever we're able to put things together into a greater wholeness, and see the many parts working as one, we are witnessing love in action.

Programmed into the deepest cells of our being, love is felt by the infant child and the new mother from the moment of birth. Love sustains us through life's travails and triumphs. It cries at the gates of mystery when we release a loved one's hand with their last breath.

These moments are profound, indelible and essential. They give life meaning. Whenever we find love, feel love, create or express love, we tap into an essence greater than our individual being, holding us in grace as elements of something larger.

We crave love like breath, which provides yet another metaphor. Air, as the sacred element associated with the heart chakra, is an invisible field that surrounds us, while supplying every breath. Divine love also envelops us. It is always there, but to the uninitiated remains unseen. And just as the wind reveals the invisible movements of air, demonstrations of love reveal the divine force that holds everything together in an intricate web of relationships.

Love breathes a sigh of relief whenever it is restored or expanded. Love is our next evolutionary challenge – the one that will make or break the survival of our species into the next era.

We certainly know that the human heart is opened, expanded and uplifted by an experience of love. We feel this expansion as a spiritual "Aha!" that beckons us onwards to a deeper mystery. Once love is tasted, we want that taste again and again. Like a benevolent disease, love is contagious – an open heart inspires other hearts to open and drink of this majesty. It teaches us from deep within an essential lesson about the world – that everything dances in relationship, creating ever larger wholes. From atoms to molecules, from people to planets, from stars to galaxies, we are immersed in a field of creation perfectly balanced, dancing in perpetual reciprocity.

There has never been a time in the world more urgently beseeching us to open our hearts. The intricate network of the biosphere hangs by a thread, while 65 million people wander the Earth as homeless refugees, too many of them children.

We can no longer afford the old, tired wars of you and me, us and them, this and that, instead of celebrating the amazement of each other's differences. We must no longer see Heaven and Earth as separate concepts, as if the cosmic mother and father had filed for divorce and were splitting up the property, instead of being the ultimate lovers of eternity that gave birth to everything we know.

And there has never been a time when we had such freedom to select for love. We can choose a mate whom we love, rather than an assigned partner; we can even choose to love a gender that suits our truest nature. We can increasingly opt for a profession that we love, choose to live where we love, and eat, study and play according to what we love.

Gradually, as we make the long evolutionary journey to grow up and find our power and freedom, we realize that the underlying reason we want freedom so badly is to be free to choose a life we can love.

A world chosen for love is evolution's next enterprise.

What would it take to create a world where love is the *central organizing principle*? This would be a world of balanced exchanges, which fosters collaboration over competition, webs of connection over chains of command, networks over markets, stakeholders over stockholders, an ecosystem over an ego system. It would be a world based on self-organizing principles, peer-to-peer networks of individuals serving a larger vision to create the reality we know in our hearts is possible.

Despite evidence to the contrary in our sensation-driven media, this is already happening. The largest social movement on Earth today, according to the American writer and activist Paul Hawken, is the voluntary movement of people towards humanitarian service, through countless non-governmental organizations, whose express purpose is to promote social justice, environmental stability, peace, democracy and/or the study of consciousness. This movement is global and cuts across age, race and gender. It isn't the result of a legal decree or the command of the powerful. It's arising from the hearts of people who have enough freedom to serve the common good and to save what they love.

Our technology is fostering a global connection that has never before been possible. Facebook has a larger population than any country on the planet, with over a billion people logging on daily, proving that our greatest human drive is social connection. We can watch videos of strangers on the other side of planet, and they become less strange as we learn of their plight and open our hearts in compassion. We can cry for the melting of glaciers, celebrate the ousting of a dictator, or go viral to spread new ideas and discoveries. Just as the agoras, or town squares, of ancient Greece enabled debate and gave birth to democracy, we now have global social media "ideagoras", which are bringing forth novelty, solving problems and self-selecting for collaboration.

We have long known about the power of individual love: love for our mate, our brother or sister, one's family or tribe. We are now being called to experience the power of love on a global scale, with nations coming together in planetary maturity and mutual benefit rather than breaking into self-interested fragments. What could happen if we improved the economic and social well-being of Mexico instead of building a wall across the border with the USA, for the same or less cost? What could happen if the money spent on military defence were put into education, health care or environmental protection? What could happen if the poor were educated, if women were given equality with men, if differences were celebrated, and if we worked together to solve our global problems?

Indeed, our problems today can *only* be solved through global cooperation. While ancient enemies united a population *against* something, we now have issues, such as climate change, that can unite humanity in a common cause, without having an enemy to kill. Whether we like it or not, we're becoming a global society, a global economy and a global brain. It's essential that we develop a global heart as well. Love is the sustaining value that invisibly organizes this colossal syncretism into a global awakening.

The shift from the love of power to the power of love is the evolutionary thrust of our time. Love begins in our own hearts, as we heal the hurts we have both caused and received (the Sanskrit name of the heart chakra, *Anahata,* means "unstruck" or "unhurt"). It moves through our bodies as we soften our body armour, yield to a deeper truth and relax our hard stances against each other. It's extended to us all through forgiveness and generosity, is given wings by gratitude, and ultimately finds its nest in peace.

This love is wildly creative, calling people en masse to dance together in celebration, with a new spirituality that is not dictated but co-created, to open the wings of the heart's resplendent temple. For love does not come from dreary legislation but from the heart's own wisdom, the quintessence of every spiritual philosophy that has ever existed. As we practise and pray, we are vibrating into a new configuration, so far beyond what we now have that we can barely imagine its grace-filled gifts.

For here is the certainty of the future's next adventure: love's luscious enterprise is standing with its doors wide open, offering appetizers for the banquet yet to come.

You are cordially invited.

CONTEMPLATIVE REFLECTIONS ON

Light Shining

As soul awakens and heart opens, we enter the inner planes of consciousness through the process of refining gross energy into subtle energy. As energy becomes more subtle, consciousness becomes more amplified and penetrating, and we experience its luminosity. Now, at last, we journey through an inner world of light that feeds our growing awareness of the resplendent nature of spiritual reality.

_____

In the inner reaches of your heart, a light

shines. It is a light that is eternally present.

The primordial light that shines in the heart

is the light of consciousness and the progenitor

of all light in the world.

_____

The light that shines in your heart cannot be switched on or off. It is invisible to the busy mind. Its presence cannot be felt by a fretful, self-concerned heart.

_____

The inner light of the heart shines from a place far beyond the personal self. It is beyond distinctions between light and dark or good and evil.

_____

Here in the heart is the light that shines before the world begins and long before thought arises. No wonder mystics from so many traditions emphasize the greatness and magnificence of the heart: it is the gateway to the light that has evolved all life.

_____

We are bearers of this light but so often we are unaware that it shines in the centre of our own being. Evolution's abundant creativity is sourced by this original light, expressing itself in new science, cosmology, psychology, social systems, the arts, technology and enlightened morality.

_____

Towering philosophy, intellectual brilliance and other dazzling performances of the ego have heard reports of this light but may never have experienced it. Yet the light informs intellect, insight and discovery when these attributes align themselves with it.

The light shining in your heart's core is knowledge, insight, wisdom and love as one unified presence. Such a light can never be apprehended by fragmented awareness.

_____

Behold the light that opens the luminous third eye. It is the light of the all-knowing One, guiding the evolution of all life and the involution of all souls as they return to divine Source.

_____

_____

The light that reveals itself in the heart is a light that touches. Although universal in nature, it is filled with intimate presence. It is simultaneously personal and impersonal.

_____

One of the defining aspects of this original light is its liberating power. Every idea, attitude and belief that shackles us in separation or superiority is freed from its soul-destroying confines by this light.

Falseness, self-deception and lack of integrity hide from this light. Only that which is transparent abides in eternal truth. To behold the completely transparent is difficult, because our perception is filtered by projections that constantly colour our view. When we see without those filters, we enter the Presence.

———————————————

Bathed in this all-enveloping light, the mind

sheds illusion and the heart surrenders and

worships what is real and true.

———————————————

Your heart is a portal of light. You cannot force that light to come to you. As your heart opens, be receptive. Contemplate the fact that the light is already there. We do not create the light, we simply find it. Or as a mystic might see it, the light finds us when we are at home in ourselves.

Light has a way of finding you whatever door you may have closed within yourself. Nothing can keep the light out. When the light of pure consciousness seems obscured, that is because we have stepped into an illusion.

See with the eye of the heart the light that shines in the darkness.

Embrace the suffering you have experienced but do not clutch at it, or it will eclipse the light of your heart. Worries are like heavy storm clouds blocking the sun's rays. But do not worry: clouds shed rain to teach us how the skies open and the glory of sunlight is recovered.

_____

Let the light shine. Shining is its dynamic radiant quality. It can penetrate the densest fog of resentment and resistance. It can illuminate the path forward. It is the light of Presence.

_____

Mind swings back and forth between fears and desires, hopes and regrets, and gets lost in the past or future. Mind gets caught in the swamps and fogs of illusion. The light in your heart shines only in the present where it reveals what Native American elders call the "Beauty Way".

———————————————

As soul awakens and heart opens, the light

that guides the universe shines through you.

And you enter the flow of light's creative

emergence as universal love, ceaseless

originality and cosmic playfulness.

———————————————

Light Shining

BY ERVIN LÁSZLÓ

The founder of systems theory and general evolution theory, Ervin László received the Goi Peace Prize in 2001. His work in recent years has focused on the "Akasha Paradigm", a new conception of cosmos, life and consciousness.

"The primordial light that shines in the heart is the light of consciousness and the progenitor of all light in the world." James O'Dea's words capture the essence of a scientific approach to "light shining".

The consciousness that's present in you is not a finite, limited consciousness. It's an infinite, cosmic consciousness – a reflection, a holographic resonance, of the consciousness that forms and in-forms the universe. It's present in the depth of your mind, in your heart.

This light – this consciousness – didn't begin when the universe did. It's the intelligence that gave birth to the universe. In the beginning was the Word, as the Old Testament reveals (Genesis 1.1): this was the Tao, the Brahman, the Cosmic Spirit insightful people knew the world over. We can now say, with the physicist Max Planck, that it's the cosmic intelligence that keeps the vibration of protons, neutrons and electrons together so they make up an atom. The cosmic intelligence keeps atoms together so they make up molecules, and keeps molecules together to make up living cells. It's also this intelligence that keeps the cells of your body vibrating in syntony (matched frequencies) so they make up your living brain and body, the biological template of your mind and consciousness.

This cosmic intelligence is associated with your body, but it isn't your body. It's the intelligence *of* your body. It's the light that shines forth in you, and in all things in the universe.

This light is the hologram that envelops and embraces – that in-forms – all things. It in-forms the cells and organs of your body, and it in-forms your brain and consciousness. When you enter a prayerful, meditative state, it connects you with all the beings that emerge and evolve in space and time.

You cannot receive this light, cannot communicate and commune with it, in your everyday state of consciousness. Your mind is too busy with the superficialities of daily life. You need to enter a deeper state of consciousness, one in which you can receive the wisdom of the cosmos, resonate with the intelligence that created your body and everything around you.

When you enter this state, you see with the eye of your heart. You are in-formed with the wisdom that co-evolves things in space and time.

These ideas sound spiritual, beyond the range of science and common sense, but they aren't esoteric. It isn't that common sense would have evolved on its own to embrace them: it's more that science has evolved, and continues to evolve, to in-form common sense. When you absorb the new paradigm in science – a post-materialist, integral paradigm – the wisdom that guides the evolution of all things in the universe becomes evident to you. That is the awakening addressed in this prayer.

We're living at a time when the awakening to the wisdom of the universe is manifesting in increasing numbers of people. This is a time when the light of the deepest dimension of the cosmos – the dimension scientists know as the "zero-point" or "Akashic field", or the "implicate order" – begins to penetrate the hearts of people. Without this heartfelt wisdom nothing could exist in the universe beyond inert gases floating randomly in passive space and indifferently flowing time. But it's present throughout the universe, and it's present in your body and brain. It can be recalled by your consciousness and can enter your life as a shining light that guides your every step.

At this critical point in our history, the consciousness needed to tackle the problems of our time is surfacing in the minds of a critical mass of people. This consciousness, which was known to insightful individuals for millennia, is now being rediscovered at the leading edge of the sciences. It's the consciousness we need to solve the problems that face us. As Einstein pointed out, we can't solve the critical problems of our time with the same kind of consciousness that gave birth to them.

The new consciousness opens the human mind to the vibration that created the universe 13.8 billion years ago. This vibration began to in-form the universe in the aftermath of the cosmic explosion known as the Big Bang, and has been doing so ever since. In a seemingly slow and tentative but ultimately decisive and insistently irreversible process, it has been bringing forth complex and coherent systems that interact, and in their interaction communicate, commune and co-evolve in the myriad webs of life that exist throughout this living and conscious universe.

The light that shines in your soul is the consciousness that in-forms the world. It's the holographic projection, the resonance, of consciousness at the heart of reality. Ultimately, as the great wisdom traditions have long been maintaining, the matter–energy world of space and time is the venture of beyond-spacetime cosmic consciousness to behold itself.

You can, and you need to, live up to the task and the challenge of evolving your consciousness. You're an evolved creation of the consciousness that reigns in the cosmos; in you, cosmic consciousness shines forth brightly and articulately. You're an evolved instrument of the self-creation of the consciousness of the world through the evolution of the things that *carry* the consciousness of the world.

The light that shines forth in you is cosmic and infinite. Treasure it, foster it, evolve it. It's your identity as a cosmic being, and fostering and evolving this light is the meaning of your existence. It's the task you are here to fulfil. You're here to pursue this responsibility not only in your present life, but in life after life.

You're a mortal being with an immortal consciousness. Your body perishes, but your consciousness survives. You're part of the infinite symphony of light manifesting on this planet.

As a rational as well as intuitive being, you must accept the challenge of beholding and evolving the light that shines in your heart. This is your immortal consciousness. It must grow and evolve, and in-form all life on this planet, and throughout the universe.

CONTEMPLATIVE REFLECTIONS ON

Love Flowing

Love is the uniting movement of existence. It's the ceaseless flow of life-giving power forever offering itself as the vital nourishment of all that creates wholeness and harmony. There's no place too filthy, there's no story too sordid or hopeless, for love to transform it with its beauty and healing power.

In always giving of itself, love keeps growing and expanding into eternity. In the end, love is the irresistible force that fulfils every destiny. Love is the Creator. It emerges from the light and it enters through the heart.

Love is a quality of the original light of spiritual knowledge. Love knows that we are One. And love is willing to pay the most excruciating price to show that it can never be separated from the object of its love.

Love does not market or sell itself. It offers itself as a gift. It is vastly generous and free of manipulation. It spreads solely through the mysterious power of its own vulnerability, audacity and magnificence.

Although it has many imitators, love never sets out to prove itself. Love functions through resonance, not self-assertion.

Love is ingested. It is the food of heart and soul. Your whole being opens when it is tasted. And then the taste just gets richer and deeper, and deeper and richer, until you cannot separate tears and laughter or bitter and sweet.

_____

Love does not help you to become someone in order to be yourself. It loves you so you can be yourself. Have the courage to be you, even if you have already shed a thousand smaller versions of yourself which you thought at the time were your true identity.

_____

_____

Love loves you as you without reservations

or conditions. It loves you as you are, not as

you might be or should be. It has faith in your

unfolding – even over lifetimes.

_____

Love serves the whole. It is not a partisan of the part. If you give yourself to love, you serve all beings without distinction. And you do not have to put on the mantle of any piety or professional expertise to do so.

Love comes from freedom and manifests in freedom. It can never be forced. This is the basis of the principle of spiritual attraction. When there's an absence of any kind of coercion, love offers itself freely and becomes irresistibly attractive and nourishing.

Love's creativity is boundless. It is the heart of innovation, of healing, of justice, of scientific exploration and of artistic expression. Love is pure imagination. Love will recreate the world in its own image through a culture of love that informs every aspect of human development.

_____

The mystic discovers what is real and abiding

by taking the path of love and eating the heart-

opening fruits of love along the way.

_____

If you seek to understand why we evolve, turn to love for the answer. When we understand that it is love that is leading us through natural selection processes to create an advantage for compassionate and collaborative human beings, a new science and a new social order will dawn. Let us explore a universe of consciousness and qualities – not just quantities, measures and scales.

———————————————

Beauty arouses love; and love engenders beauty. Learn to see beauty where you think there is only ugliness, and love will flow into a part of yourself you had forgotten about – one you had left abandoned, fearing that it was ugly.

———————————————

Treat love as food. Keep telling your numbness that you are starving for love. Feel its energy circulating through the heart and anywhere else it wants to go. If you get confused, remember this: lust leaves you hungry for more excitement; love fulfils.

———————————————

Let your breath be carried by love. Lean on love.

Unload your troubles. Soon there will be no weight.

———————————————

_____

Love is not a supply chain of sweet things and sentimental feelings. It is a spontaneous universal energy that cuts through false appearances, nurtures and protects the vulnerable and offers its life in the cause of beauty and truth.

_____

Surrender to love's power to lay bare life's essentials. Bathe in love's truth: it is only your own self that separates you from love's infinite radiance – where your dark secrets will inevitably evaporate in its forgiving light and tender warmth.

_____

Love is where human desire meets divine will. This is where we grow and where we feel the burning away of resistance. Give yourself to the flames.

_____

——————————————————————

Love is the only form of abundance that really matters.

——————————————————————

Great science does not seek to deny love as if it were something that blurs objective truth. True inquiry explores from the ground of love, which combines humility, reverence, dedication and awe.

Out of the primordial light shining in the heart comes all the love we need. To fulfil our human destiny we enter the flow and become love. Planetary civilization will evolve in great leaps as we woo the future with our longing for the politics of love, the economy of love, the religion of love and the myriad forms of love rising out of our accelerated connectivity.

Love Flowing

BY KABIR HELMINSKI

An author, educator and retreat leader, Kabir Helminski is a translator of the works of the 13th-century Sufi poet Rumi and a Shaikh of the Mevlevi Order. He is also co-founder and co-director of The Threshold Society (sufism.org).

If you've ever fallen completely in love, you know that in love we come alive. In the state called falling in love, two people give the juice of attention to each other in such a way that each feels valued and, even more significantly, *recognized*. When we're in the state of giving and receiving love, all of life takes on a special glow. Lovers listen deeply to each other: they hear each other's every word. It's such an intense experience that people can even become addicted to its heady rush.

As beautiful as this experience is, it isn't the most mature, enduring or beautiful kind of love. But it does reveal to us the power of love to bring happiness, to enliven and transform.

Instead of such fleeting highs, is it possible to know a more lasting, constant and true transformation? It's difficult enough to find this and sustain it with one person. How can we love in widening circles of human beings? Ultimately, how might we love the Source of existence itself?

These may seem like excessively exalted and idealistic questions, given the lives that many of us face day by day. I don't know if I'd have even been interested in such questions before I was touched by the experience of wider, deeper love. This didn't come through my high-school sweetheart, nor did it come, at first, through any romantic relationship. To my astonishment it came through a simple grandfather-like man from Turkey in whose presence I felt immediately accepted and loved. But it wasn't a love that felt personal: it wasn't about *me*. It was as if I found myself, quite unexpectedly, in a different universe: love's universe.

In what sense is love a "Path"?

The answer to this question lies in understanding the cosmic context in which we exist – namely, a universe of love. Not only is God Love, as we have so often been told, but Love is literally both the cause and the purpose of all existence. The great Turkish Sufi mystic Yunus Emre said, "The vast universe was created from just a spark of Love."

Love is the cause in so far as it's an expression of the creative power that brought everything into existence. It's the purpose in so far as all of existence is revealing and promoting the qualities of love. In other words, the most urgent fact of existence may be this: love loves to make itself known to us.

The exploration of love, inwardly or in discussion with others, is simultaneously intellectual, emotional, psychological and spiritual. It's ultimately spiritual because love is profoundly related to the nature of reality itself. To explore the nature of love is to come to understand its absolute importance for us as the fulfilment of a need, its relationship with beauty, its power to awaken new perceptions, its transformative effect on us, and ultimately how it leads to a perception of truth itself.

Spiritual love has a cognitive function: it transforms perception. The world looks different to a lover:

To the Prophet, this world is plunged in glorification of God,
while to many it looks inanimate.
To his eye this world is filled with abundant love;
to the eyes of others it is inert and lifeless.
To his eye, valley and hill are in fluid motion:
he hears subtle discourses from sod and bricks.
To the vulgar, this whole world is a dead thing in chains:
I have never seen a veil of blindness more amazing than this.

(Rumi, Mathnawi IV, 3532–5)

And there are many levels to this experience of divine love. Love makes possible a transformation of perception and being, because love is itself the highest truth, the very nature of reality. When we're more in the state of love, we're closer to the truth, and therefore our perceptions are less distorted.

I don't know of a magical technique that can miraculously create love. Love, itself, *is* the magical technique, the greatest transforming power in existence.

> By love, the bitter becomes sweet;
> by love, copper becomes gold;
> by love, the dregs become clear;
> by love, the dead become living;
> by love, the king becomes a slave.
> From knowledge, love grows.
> Has stupidity ever placed someone on such a throne?
> (Rumi, *Mathnawi* II, 1529–32)

This ultimate perception of truth has been described by some mystics as a merging of self with the infinite.

LOVE IS A FIRE AND EGO IS ITS FUEL

While there are many understandings of love, I would like to propose this one: conscious love is the degree of relationship between the human lover and Divine Beloved. And if this relationship is allowed to fulfil itself, it will result in harmony, communion and even union itself. But before we go there, we should take a look at what stands in the way of love: namely, egoism, by which I mean all the motivations, strategies and defences of the "false self".

Negativity, blame and judgement are like filters that colour and distort what we see. Fear, suspicion or lust can affect how we see others.

All negative states are like shadows that vanish when the light of love appears. When we can see another human being with the eyes of love, we not only free ourselves from distorted perception, but also help to transform that other person. When recognized by love, people are more likely to drop the mask of the false self. This may be why we feel more ourselves in the presence of a holiness that doesn't judge or blame; we may also feel a positive sense of shame and be in awe of the mercy extended to us.

To diminish egoism is not to destroy a sense of "I", that identity without which we could not even relate or function, but rather to *purify* the sense of I-ness. If we can rid the essential self of its distortions, prejudices, vanity, self-righteousness, defensiveness and unreasonable fears, then we'll be left with a wholly different sense of who we are.

> My soul is a furnace
> happy with the fire.
> Love, too, is a furnace,
> and egoism is its fuel.
>
> (Rumi, *Mathnawi* II, 1376–7)

All of these pathologies of the false self are like false-I's that deserve to dissolve and die.

> For lovers, there is a dying in every moment:
> truly, the dying of lovers is not of one kind.
> The lover has been given two hundred lives
> from the Soul of Guidance;
> each instant she sacrifices another.
> For each life she gives, she receives ten:
> as it is said in the Qur'an "ten like unto them".*
>
> (Rumi, *Mathnawi* III, 3834–5)

So what is the corrective to all these pathologies of egoism? Essentially, it's the light of Presence, the awakened consciousness which inherently reflects the cosmic field of Love. Presence is a state of comprehensive self-awareness

---

* Qur'an: Surah Hud 11.13. The meaning is that whatever we give or sacrifice is returned tenfold.

through which we experience the cosmic field of Love. Just by being present with an open heart, we enter into this powerful force-field in which the false-I's dissolve. We stop defending these false-I's, simply by dissolving the resentment and defensiveness that underlie them. What has to die is not the sense of self, but the rationalizations and justifications that create a *false* self. What has to die is the vanity that maintains our illusions. Furthermore, when we no longer sustain the blame and judgement of others that sustain the false self, we enter a realistic humility. This humility has nothing to do with having a low estimate of ourselves: rather, it is our awareness of our dependence on the cosmic field of Love.

> Love is whispering into my ear,
> "To be a prey is better than to be a hunter.
> Make yourself My fool:
> renounce the high estate of the sun and become a speck!
> Come dwell at My door and be homeless:
> don't pretend to be a candle, be a moth,
> so you may taste the savour of Life
> and contemplate the sovereignty hidden in servanthood."
>
> (Rumi, *Mathnawi* V, 411–14)

In our tradition, the word "lover" is used to describe the seeker. The lover is therefore someone quite different from the nominal believer. For the nominal believer, the Divine is something to refer to in times of need, in the great passages of life – birth, marriage, death. However, the lover longs to be continually in awareness of the Divine Presence as Love.

Lovers have a very direct relationship with the Divine. For them the Divine is the ultimate Beauty itself. They are more passionate about this than any teenager in the first throes of infatuation.

> For lovers, the only lecturer
> is the beauty of the Beloved:
> their only book and lecture and lesson is that Face.
> Outwardly they are silent,
> but their penetrating remembrance rises
> to the high throne of their Friend.
> Their only lesson is enthusiasm, whirling and trembling,
> not the precise points of law.
>
> (Rumi, *Mathnawi* III, 3847–9)

The opening to love is done through the heart, which is a cognitive instrument. In other words, it's through the heart that we glimpse the Real by means of the Light of Love.

> Listen, open a window to God
> and begin to delight yourself

by gazing upon Him through the opening.
The business of love is to make that window in the heart,
for the breast is illumined by the beauty of the Beloved.
Gaze incessantly on the face of the Beloved!
Listen, this is in your power, my friend!

(Rumi, *Mathnawi* VI, 3095–7)

The spiritual lover says, "My religion is to be kept alive by Love." Love's journey is the journey of every human being through all the levels of being. There's no journey more true, more real, more important. And, in the end, there's no greater love than love with no object, for then you have become Love itself. Love flowing ceaselessly.

CONTEMPLATIVE REFLECTIONS ON

Wounds Dissolving

Wounds feed on wounds. Over time, if not dissolved, wounds form a constellation of anger, hurt and recrimination which implode in self-destruction or explode in violence to others. We live in a world of wound contagion.

Wounds are often transmitted to others and can be sustained for generations, wreaking havoc in cycle after cycle of abuse and carnage. But these cycles can be skilfully interrupted when there is a commitment to the kind of truth that allows people to express their deepest pain and dream a new story together.

Wounding can help to ignite soul awakening and heart opening when it spurs us to explore what really constitutes lasting truth, abiding love and true compassion.

Wounds grow like mould in the dark field of repressed energy. Repression itself can spread as a contagion in the collective unconscious. Seeing the mind's distortion and remembering how our energy was originally seeking an ideal helps to dissolve the toxin. There was always good to begin with.

Forgiveness has the power to dissolve wounds.

It is the bridge to reconciliation and new life.

It releases attachment to being the injured

party. Forgiveness refuses to be dominated by

perpetual resentment.

_____

Non-judgement and heart-centred listening thaw

frozen layers of injury, isolation and resentment.

We freeze over when we are not heard.

_____

_____

Unconditional love is a true salve for the

wounds of rejection and the scar tissue of

neglect. It allows us to breathe in acceptance

and melt resistance.

_____

Punitive and vengeful justice add wound upon wound. Restorative justice heals. Humanity's future requires justice that seeks to restore communal health and heal broken trust.

Prejudice manifests as hatred of others but its origin is the wound of damaged self-esteem. Prejudice is dissolved when we see that there is nothing inadequate in ourselves. When we ourselves are whole, no one else can be regarded as inferior.

Wounds can lie dormant in the mind, self-imprisoned and guarded by fear. Fear turns to rage, and rage takes on many disguises. Rage preaches from pulpits, feeds the coffers of politicians and drives around in sleek limousines. Then one day the pain of oppressor and oppressed meet face to face, often creating more wounds. But with skilful means all wounds can be dissolved.

The healer knows how to liberate the pain that is trapped inside our wounds. It begins with melting all that has been frozen by the guardians of numbness.

The wounded healer surrenders all attachment to protracted suffering and has the courage to step into the unknown and even to face more wounding. Such a healer sets the precedent for total surrender to using all experiences for one's own spiritual growth and the well-being of others.

Once abuse or victimization has ceased, if any part of you identifies itself as a victim, feel the pain and let it go. This is frontline work towards spiritual and social change. Let the release of suffering spur insight, understanding and compassion, as well as the fresh energy you will need to be your most creative self.

If you have difficulty seeing past condemnation of perpetrators, focus your attention on their hidden wounds. Use empathic power to call repressed wounding out of hiding. This does not require a whitewashing of accountability: it requires a commitment to addressing the causes of abuse.

_____

In the presence of light shining and love flowing,

wounds lose their self-destructive power. They

dissolve in the arms of peace, because the mind's

gyrations simply come to an end.

_____

Wounds Dissolving

BY MICHAEL A SINGER

The author of the New York Times *bestsellers* The Untethered Soul *and* The Surrender Experiment, *Michael A Singer founded the Temple of the Universe in 1975 as a yoga and meditation centre for all faiths.*

As we pass through life, everything we experience comes in through our senses and leaves an impression on our minds and hearts. If these experiences are fairly neutral, like the white lines on the road, they come in, make enough of an impression for us to experience them, and then they simply pass through. However, if we give these mental impressions power because we fear or desire them, then they stay, trapped in the mind. But they don't stay on their own power; they stay because we keep them – we hold them inside ourselves. We hold uncomfortable impressions inside because we don't want to fully experience them. We inwardly push them away from our seat of consciousness. Yet the act of pushing them away actually keeps them locked within us. Likewise, if we like or need something, we don't want the impression to go away – so we mentally cling to it. In both cases, what we keep builds up inside of us and actually blocks our energy flow. It is like rocks that get put into a stream. The stream was flowing evenly, but when the rock is put in, it creates eddies and currents, and maybe even rapids.

These things we collect over the course of our lives create disturbance within us. There's no rock you can put inside a flowing stream that does not disturb the flow. These disturbances within us come back up regularly. If we see something that reminds us of what we held inside, even if it is just tangentially related, all the original feelings and thoughts start to resurface. When this happens, either we tend to push them back down, or we try to create thoughts that will neutralize the inner disturbance. In both cases, these past impressions are running our lives. Because we have to deal with these disturbances, we miss the reality of the present moment. This is why *mindfulness* is a spiritual practice instead of our natural state.

In yoga, these stored past experiences are called *samskaras*. These samskaras, especially the negative ones, are like wounds we carry within us. When they are stimulated, they can come up with great pain. They were stored with pain, and they will come up again with pain. Even the positive things that happen to us, since we want them to happen again, can form the foundation for deep disappointment and make us feel wounded. Ultimately, everything we hold inside ourselves about the past that is charged with our personal sense of fear or desire creates wounds that will come back up and disturb us over the course of our lives.

Most people, because they don't understand what's going on, try to manipulate and control the outside world so that it won't bring up the disturbances that are uncomfortable to them. So the wounds of our past are now running our present. And if we're not careful, they will run the rest of our lives.

What spirituality is about, regardless of what path we follow or what techniques we use, is removing these blockages. As we remove them, we are removing the potential for being wounded by past experiences. After all, the world cannot wound us. The world is an experience that comes in to us, and we learn and grow from it. If it has wounded us, that's because we've resisted the experience and held it inside. If it's no longer going on outside, why is it still creating disturbance inside? The answer is: because we did not let it go. Admittedly, it can be difficult letting some painful experiences pass through. But you're always better off permitting the past to be an experience you had, and then letting it go. It will still become part of you; you don't lose anything by not resisting it. You actually become a greater being because of every experience you have.

Thus, the removal of past blockages is the same as the removal of wounds. But how does one go about removing the blockages? One must first reach the point of understanding that these blockages are the cause of all our problems, both personally and collectively. Because we are not comfortable within ourselves, we are driven to manipulate the world around us, which leads to mistreatment of others and even wars. If we're able to let go of the past impressions held inside us, the world coming in through our senses can be a very fulfilling experience. The sunset is beautiful, the sunrise is beautiful, rain is beautiful, snow is beautiful, cold is beautiful, heat is beautiful. All sorts of things are just experiences that we're having. If we are willing to experience them and let go, we start to appreciate life. When we approach life with respect, we start to see the entire majesty of creation expressing itself in what's unfolding before us. If you neither like nor dislike, you start to be in awe that things even exist. Everything passing before you took 13.8 billion years to get there. This is how a spiritual being sees the current moment. But that cannot happen while we're holding on to these past inner wounds. How we perceive the world is simply the reflection of what's going on inside of us.

Fortunately, without a single exception, all our stored impressions from the past can be released. If we are willing to let them come up and not push them back down again, they will pass away by themselves. There is a natural system of healing within your energy flow. It is no different than with your physical body. The physical body has a miraculous immune system that works day and night on its mission of purification. The same thing is true with your mind and your heart. The impressions you have stored inside, which are causing disturbances in the energy flow, need to be removed. This energy flow, which has been given different names by different cultures (*shakti, chi, spirit, flow*), is trying to push the blockages out of the way. The only reason it can't is because you won't let it. You don't want to experience the pain, the disturbance that comes with purification. A wise person treats the process exactly as if they were trying to stop smoking, or break any other habit. You'll have to go through a period when it's uncomfortable. But at the end of that period, you'll be free.

You must learn to consciously work with the blockages by permitting the energy flow to push them up so they can be released. If the world reminds you of something that was painful in the past, that's good because it gives you an opportunity to let it go. If it wasn't stored in there, it wouldn't be coming up. You must decide: do I want to spend my life avoiding these blockages, or do I want to master the art of letting them go?

A wise person just keeps letting go. You just willingly relax in the face of the disturbance and allow the wounds to dissolve. Over time, what you'll find is that a number of things happen. First, you'll become less reactive to the reality unfolding in front of you. You'll start to appreciate, honour and respect creation, instead of being afraid of it or needing something from it. Second, because you've removed these blockages from your energy flow, you'll start to feel a tremendous upward rush of energy rising within you. This flow is intoxicating and extremely beautiful. Where there used to be fear and anxiety, now there's joy, enthusiasm and passion for everything.

This flow of energy, because it's been freed from having to fight its way through the blockages, is a gift that you've earned through the inner work you've done. The dissolving of wounds is not just a non-negative, it ends up becoming a tremendous positive. Ultimately, that beautiful flow of inner energy becomes your whole life. It becomes so strong that you cannot keep yourself from falling into it. Yet life continues to unfold in front of you, and you deal with it. But you deal with it with joy and enthusiasm, not with fear and the need to protect yourself.

In the end, you will see that the dissolving of wounds is the entire spiritual path. The only reason we are separated from the Universal is because these blockages have separated us. Once the blockages are gone, all the waters merge together again.

CONTEMPLATIVE REFLECTIONS ON

Peace Radiating

There cannot be peace until we end our rebellion against Holy Mother Nature and until we recover the ancestral knowledge of our kinship with Nature and the family of all beings. Nature is a manifestation of peace radiating for all life.

Peace is the radiance that emanates in the roots of every being. It radiates infinite appreciation for the gift of life and carries the harmonic codes of all existence from the heart of the universe.

_____

Peace is both stillness and movement. It is

ceaseless freshness and complete renewal

gifted to us in states of prayer, contemplation,

nourishing relationships and selfless service,

and by embodying courage and conscience.

_____

_____

Peace is the doorway to the sacred mystery of human transformation and to understanding the spiritual plan for humanity.

_____

———————————————

Peace is devoid of any passivity. But it is sun and moon – both active and receptive.

———————————————

Keep your conscience keenly attentive to live in attunement with your own evolving moral imagination. The world is full of moral dilemmas, so listen with confidence to the voice of your own higher self. Always be willing to reconsider your point of view. Know that you have been asked to walk the path of essence, even when cold reason might try to block your deeper instinct. Peace calls for participation all the way through, from the inner canvas of the soul to the deep ecology of fully embodied communities manifesting social transformation.

Any action that begins at the core of your being

unites with the source of all being. Look for that

point of ignition between the local self and the

more universal self. Whether your first gesture is

to still your mind, beat a drum, raise your voice

or cross the threshold of an old fear, celebrate

your choice to leave passivity behind and

embrace creative action.

The path to world peace is the path of connecting the disconnected. Even when we think we see the whole, we have a partial view. So make every point of contact a quality connection. In a world of interconnections you never know what difference this will make – it might be substantial.

———————————

Peace is always giving: giving voice and giving silence; giving presence and giving space; giving respect and giving support. But more than anything, peace gives creativity the courage to evolve beyond every form of resistance.

———————————

_____

Peace is acutely receptive. It is able to receive

hurt, pain and blame with equanimity, and

remain deeply attuned to the suffering of others.

_____

———————————————

Peace smiles with serenity because it knows

what it knows.

———————————————

_____

Peace is joyful self-sacrifice. This kind of sacrifice is not self-destruction. It is a conscious choice to act out of a higher principle of inclusion that transcends self-interest.

_____

_____

Peace does not withdraw in contemplation. It engages destructive forces, through empathy, moral clarity, courage and mindfulness.

_____

_____

Peace never surrenders to the peevish certainties

of violent minds. It wrestles with doubt while

constantly exploring what is real and true.

Peace knows that some truths are constant

and some are evolving.

_____

_____

True peace is justice. Economic justice, ecological

justice and social justice are all contained in a

vision of peace that stretches from deep within the

soul to its full expression in global peace and the

correction of all systemic wrongs.

_____

_____

Peace is potent, fecund and fertile. It gives life. But it begins with creatively facing down oppression in the here and now from a place within that is dazzlingly alive and free. That is why peace is the axis of what our ancestors called the "great circle of life".

_____

_____

Peace is not the absence of war. It is the pervasive presence of compassionate connection.

_____

Peace thrives when conflict is allowed to surface in healthy ways. Peace never stifles dissent.

_____

Peace guides us through dialogue to the higher mind, which sees beyond polarized distinctions. Dia means through; logos is the higher mind. Dia-logos or dialogue occurs when we commune with each other in such a way as to access our highest wisdom together.

_____

Peace does not have a separate programme or ideological platform. Peace is a reflection of a whole system of planetary ecology and universal principles of harmony and balance which we disrupt at great peril to ourselves.

Know that you are at peace and smile all the way through. Notice when you are just wearing a smile, in contrast to the times when it radiates out from the heart, lighting up a soul-to-soul encounter with another.

Remember that wounds, even the persistent ones,

eventually dissolve. Peace prevails.

You listen to insult and argument. Why not listen for peace? True listening requires silence in the mind, within an open field of perceptive attention and bonding. Healing the greater collective field of transmitted wounds can only occur in the world when leaders practise authentic listening.

Peace is active, not passive. Consider how you can be its vigilant and proactive witness and its creative instrument. You do not have to run out into the streets to begin this work. Start by addressing the conflict zones in your own head and heart. But do not stop there.

_____

Peace activates subtle energy and subtle power.

It does not use force. Let the subtle power of

peace be what you breathe when you step into

boisterous and antagonistic environments.

Become a subtle activist.

_____

Be truth. Speak your truth without violence.

Peace is a way of life but it is also strategic.

Check to see if some part of you is cringing in

a corner; if so, stand up, to the full stretch of

your being. Non-violent communication teaches

you how to listen and also how to be heard.

Deep relaxation is important but should not be confused with peace. Peace is a resonance of enlightening call and enlightened response, which keeps you on the growing edge of a consciousness that is based on whole-Earth thinking and is also service-oriented.

_____

The mind chatters incessantly because it is

voraciously hungry and starved of real substance.

When it learns to commune with heart and soul,

it finds that its real food is peace. When fed by a

vision of peace, we develop a genuine enthusiasm

for collaboration with others.

_____

Peace on Earth radiates from sharing, not from ownership. We need to share spiritual wisdom and cultural insight. We also need to share the technologies of social connectivity and collaborate to build the sharing economy.

_____

Peace is the non-dual essence of soul awakening.

I come from peace; to peace I shall return. This

journey through lifetimes, witnessing cruelty,

oppression and war, has irrevocably confirmed

for a growing multitude that peace is the way of

all awakened souls.

_____

_____

Soul awakens to manifest original peace in the hearts of a new humanity. We move inexorably beyond suffering to practise the art of fearless celebration.

_____

Peace Radiating

BY MONA POLACCA

A Havasupai, Hopi and Tewa Native American, Mona Polacca is a recognized wisdom carrier and a member of the International Council of Thirteen Indigenous Grandmothers.

Peace is the radiance that emanates in the roots of every being. It radiates infinite appreciation for the gift of life and carries the harmonic codes of all existence from the heart of the universe.

My dear relatives, you are the gift of life, you are the blessing of the thread that binds us to the past generations of your ancestry and the generations that are yet to come, the ones we will not see.

I embrace you as beautiful relatives of the world. For this is the Hopi way of greeting, with an open hand to show that I come in peace to those from other nations. The word "Hopi" means peace.

Peace is both stillness and movement. It is ceaseless freshness and renewal ...

There are moments in your daily life as you grow when you will find yourself looking into the great sky, seeing its limitless presence.

Peace is the doorway to the sacred mystery of human transformation and to understanding the spiritual plan for humanity.

Every day you will greet the blessing of the great mystery as you walk out of your home. There before you is the blessing of a new day. You may open your heart, mind and spirit to receive the teachings which will give you the understanding of the gifts that are in store for you throughout the day.

You begin by exercising gratitude for the life-giving elements: the water, the air, the fire (sun) and Mother Earth.

Peace is always giving: giving voice and giving silence; giving presence and giving space ...

If you take a moment to be conscious of your well-being, you will realize that within yourself is a wonderful energy that will bring to you an experience of understanding that will soothe your soul, allowing your entire being to be engulfed by the flow of the energy called peace.

Peace is not the absence of war. It is the pervasive presence of compassionate connection.

In peace we listen more and have greater patience, finding solutions more readily instead of keeping the fight alive.

Let us create an internal shift from living in fear and disconnection to peace, connection and harmony, regardless of what the external circumstances of our lives may look like.

Peace is a reflection of a whole system of planetary ecology and universal principles of harmony and balance which we disrupt at great peril to ourselves.

Looking back at Earth from 200 miles up in space, divisions do not exist, and it is abruptly clear that we are one family on one Earth. This basic realization, as simple as it is, has profound implications. If we recognize that all people, animals and plants, even forests and fish, are our relatives, then we are guided to act in a way that is life-sustaining, and our worldview is more open and inclusive of all life and all being.

As we awaken to the essence of peace within, we meet allies and mentors to guide us, and if we make a conscious effort to listen to our elders, we will ultimately enjoy peace in our lives.

The key is to know that within us all exist the conditions for creativity and grace to descend. Now is the time of awakening, when we become aware of our connections and our fundamental relation to each other. This is truly the time to be aware of our existence in this world and what it means to be human.

The fact of the matter is that we do not exist independently: the hurt of one is the hurt of all. Peace, which is the honour of one, is also the honour of all.

May Peace be with you.

Here is a beautiful Hopi peace prayer:

Great Spirit and all unseen, this day we pray and ask You for guidance, humbly we ask You to help us and fellow men to have recourse to peaceful ways of life, because of uncontrolled deceitfulness by humankind. Help us all to love, not hate one another.

We ask You to be seen in an image of Love and Peace. Let us be seen in beauty, the colours of the rainbow. We respect our Mother, the planet, with our loving care, for from Her breast we receive our nourishment.

Let us not listen to the voices of the two-hearted, the destroyers of mind, the haters and self-made leaders, whose lusts for power and wealth will lead us into confusion and darkness.

Seek visions always of world beauty, not violence, not battlefields.

It is our duty to pray always for harmony between man and earth, so that the earth will bloom once more. Let us show our emblem of love and goodwill for all life and land.

Pray for the House of Glass, for within it are minds clear and pure as ice and mountain streams. Pray for the great leaders of nations in the House of Mica who in their own quiet ways help keep the Earth in balance.

We pray the Great Spirit that one day our Mother Earth will be purified into a healthy peaceful one. Let us sing for strength of wisdom with all nations for the good of all people. Our hope is not yet lost, purification must be to restore the health of our Mother Earth for lasting peace and happiness.

Techqua Ikachi – for Land and Life!*

---

* This prayer, published in *Hotevilla: Hopi Shrine of the Covenant – Microcosm of the World* by Thomas E Mails and Dan Evehema, was offered by representatives of the Hopi Nation at the "House of Glass/Mica" – that is, the United Nations.

15 Key Spiritual Concepts

1 Consciousness evolves toward enlightenment, via soul awakening

From a spiritual perspective, consciousness unfolds in developmental phases until it flowers in full realization or enlightenment. In the journey to its flowering, human consciousness has a decisive pivot point when it is thrust inwards in self-revelation. Once this occurs, an individual shifts away from a life direction dependent on external events and opens more and more to a conscious inner life guided by love and wisdom and the passionate quest to be an embodiment of abiding truth. We call this axis of transformation "soul awakening". Religion, with its adherence to a set of unvarying instructions, is designed to guide us beyond the most dense layers of consciousness and coarse aspects of human behaviour. Spirituality is more spontaneous, and represents the entrance to the subtle planes of consciousness where deep awakening occurs.

2 Consciousness pervades the cosmos

Consciousness is a unified field. While we have distinctly different thoughts and ideas from each other, we all share consciousness, which makes individual thinking possible. As water is to biological life, so consciousness is to creation.

Consciousness creates everything, and it is not restricted to humans. Consciousness in its pure, knowing and powerful aspect is the source and powerhouse of evolution.

3 We learn and grow through a succession of lives

Reincarnation makes it possible to learn and grow from contrasting life experiences. Every experience stamps its impression on life after life. We need a wide spectrum of experiences to overcome the conditioning effect of any given impression. Reincarnation eventually gives us the 360-degree perspective we need to see reality clearly. We come through the whole story of wealth and poverty, sickness and health, success and failure until we discover what truly matters in eternity.

4 We humans are one with all of life: there is no separation

The human genome is the book of life. DNA is part of the shared weave of all life on Earth. We arrive at full human adaptation and evolved consciousness as an integral part of creation, not as something separate from other living things. When humanity reaches a full appreciation of this primary truth, it will enter the spiritual phase of its journey toward collective soul awakening, social justice and ecological balance.

5 Awakening begins when the heart opens to love

We evolve spiritually through the opening of the heart. The inner space of the heart is as wide as the universe itself. We tend to crowd the heart with self-concern, longing, fantasy, worry and fear. The great journey begins when the heart remains open despite all these things and when love is experienced as a universal force of connection with all life. The heart is key to experiencing wholeness in ourselves and oneness with all creation.

6 Indivisible light shines within us all

When we find the light that shines in the heart, we discover that it's the primordial and original light. We are conditioned into pairing light with darkness, but this light is indivisible. Mystics refer to it as luminous darkness. This is the light that embraces all: the light of the inner sight of consciousness itself.

7 Healing the world means letting go of our hurts

Being attached to our own wounds and grounding our identity in our sense of ourselves as victims are a source of terrible suffering and great violence. Dissolving the toxic rationale that perpetuates resentment, self-pity, hate and rage is the most fundamental assignment for bringing healing and peace into society.

8 Unconditional love harmonizes the world

Much of what passes for love in our world is really affection, attraction, admiration, co-dependence, security or sentimental indulgence. From a spiritual point of view, love is so much more than these things. It connects but does not set any preconditions or impose any limits. Love unites through freedom: it cannot be forced on anyone. It expresses itself through selfless service. Love flows because it is self-generating and unconditional. Love's tent is all-inclusive. Love sees the essential beauty in every being, even though that beauty is invariably blocked by harsh judgements and divisive and dogmatic thinking.

9 Planes of consciousness rise by degrees from physical to enlightened

There are different planes of consciousness. The intensity of the physical plane is so strong that consciousness gets entangled in matter. The result is that we fall into the trap of thinking we are essentially physical beings. Spiritual progress occurs when consciousness shifts upwards into subtle energy, whereby it becomes free of any kind of material domination. There are many levels of subtle consciousness before the planes of purified mind and perfect insight begin.

10 Non-dual consciousness will heal the self and the world

Duality functions in an effective and necessary way at one level of consciousness. We have opposites not only in physics and the laws of nature, but also in morality. There's right and wrong, there's attraction and repulsion. But without compromising duality, the higher levels of consciousness lead us to non-duality on our journey home to absolute oneness. When we see from a non-dual perspective, the scientific truth that everything is interrelated and interdependent becomes an existential reality. To imagine families, communities, nations and ultimately a global civilization emerging out of non-dual consciousness is a vision to inspire us all.

11 Peace is a way of being, not a resolution of conflicts

Peace is a practice that comes from learning to merge with a state of being that is itself radiantly and dynamically peaceful. Peace is a central code of existence: we evolve into peace. With peace comes faith and trust in each other. In order to live the way of peace we must learn how to *be* peace and how to *practise* peace. From the beginning we must teach our children how to breathe peace, how to speak peace and how to build peace in the midst of conflict and turmoil.

12 True wisdom grows from prayer rather than intellect

Our evolution is not a linear progression. In every leap forward we meet setbacks and challenges until we fully integrate what needs to be learned. The more we evolve, the greater the challenges we face, but all the time we're becoming better equipped to deal with them. What's needed, however, is not a one-directional kind of learning, but rather a deep collective communion with higher consciousness itself. Out of such a process comes deep coherence and wisdom. To reach this level, intellect alone is not enough. In addition, we need to be prayerful and contemplative. Our prayers, embedded in our deepest longing, have always expressed our greatest wisdom. Today we need prayers that harmonize with what we know to be true and with the emerging frontiers of knowledge. We need prayers that invoke our highest aspiration. The prayers of a transforming global humanity communing together will lead us home to peace.

13 Compassion, based on love and understanding, is deeply healing

We live at a time when great compassion is needed. There can't be compassion without understanding. Compassion is never an abstract idea.

There can't be compassion for the deeply resentful without understanding how their resentment springs from dashed hopes and aspirations. There can't be compassion for those infected with unbridled materialism and greed without understanding how they're rooted in emotional emptiness. There can't be compassion for addicts without understanding how anyone can get entangled in cycles of biochemical highs and lows or how we can escape these by activating the higher will.

We can't have compassion for people incapable of caring or empathy without understanding what it means never to have experienced unconditional love. We can't have compassion for criminals and other wrongdoers without understanding how goodness can be degraded by degrees.

We can't have compassion for racial or religious bigots until we understand how wounds repressed in the unconscious take on the guise of righteousness and superiority. We can't have compassion for people consumed with hatred until we really understand how only love can triumph over hate.

14 Moral failings, challenged heroically, are great opportunities for growth

For each of the seven deadly sins (pride, lust, sloth, greed, anger, gluttony and envy) there's symbolically a separate "gate of hell" – and also a unique opportunity for evolutionary learning. Those who succumb to one of these so-called vices inhabit the psychological and energetic hell-realm pertaining to that vice. One of two things may happen then. The person may become a "demonic" attractor, their addiction luring others into the flaw that dominates their psyche; or they may engage in a heroic and redemptive struggle to overcome their problem.

The seven deadly sins have the power to cause deep harm to the self, but there's a truly inspiring and hopeful dimension to the work of overcoming any form of vicious addiction. You could say this is frontline evolutionary endeavour. Any time any one of us commits to peeling away the layers of behaviour that hold us down and impede us from being our true selves, we are creating a context for evolutionary learning. When this happens, one of the seven gates of hell opens just a crack, until one day, after sufficient people have spiritually liberated themselves from a particular vice, we will have learned as a species all we need to learn, and that gate will never close again.

Those who stand in judgement of the proud, the greedy, the slothful and so on, should ask themselves if they've done their part to open one of the "gates of hell" or any difficult evolutionary learning curve and help to give birth to a new humanity. Ultimately, as spiritual masters attest, no soul shall be left behind.

15 Prayer can be listening, as well as asking or giving thanks

Science confirms that when we listen, something quite amazing happens: we actually change the biochemistry of our body; and the deeper we listen, the more profound the change. Deep listening stills the fight-or-flight response to fear in the mid-brain, and can orchestrate mental calmness and heart coherence.

But even more amazingly, your own listening can have many of the same effects on the person you are listening to. Heartfelt listening seems to create a field that draws us into greater and greater resonance. You have probably, on occasions, felt that you were deeply communing with another simply by the act of listening. Taking this idea further, we can see that the political landscape could be utterly transformed by deep listening.

When listening is truly mutual, it can be not only emotionally rewarding and healing but also spiritually uplifting.

We tend to think of prayer as supplication or affirmation: we're either calling for something or singing praises. But try prayer as listening: listening for your own truest voice to rise out of inner stillness; listening for mysterious guidance to form as deep intuition; listening to both the suffering of humanity and its irrepressible quest for justice and joy; and listening as a form of touching and tasting the ineffable.

Contributor Biographies

FOREWORD WRITER

Lynne McTaggart

One of the central voices in the new consciousness movement, Lynne McTaggart is the award-winning author of seven books, including the worldwide bestsellers *The Field*, *The Intention Experiment*, *The Bond* and the forthcoming *The Power of Eight*. Her books are now available in some 30 languages. Lynne is also the architect of the Intention Experiment, a web-based "global laboratory" which was prominently featured in the plotline of Dan Brown's blockbuster *The Lost Symbol*. As editorial director of *What Doctors Don't Tell You* (www.wddty.com), she is also responsible for one of the world's most highly praised health magazines, now published in 14 countries.

A resident of London, Lynne is an accomplished international speaker on the science of spirituality. Her documentaries on this subject include *What the Bleep?! Down the Rabbit Hole*, *I Am* and *The Abundance Factor*. She is consistently listed as one of the world's 100 most spiritually influential people. Her website is lynnemctaggart.com.

Contributors of Guest Essays
(in alphabetical order)

Kabir Helminski

Kabir Helminski is a translator of the works of Rumi and other Sufi mystics and, since 1990, a Shaikh of the Mevlevi Order (which can be traced back to Jalaluddin Rumi). He is also co-director of The Threshold Society (sufism.org) and director/founder of the Baraka Institute (barakainstitute.org), two non-profit educational foundations that have developed programmes to provide a structure for practice and study within Sufism and spiritual psychology. From 2000 to 2010 he was co-director of the Book Foundation (thebook.org) publishing the work of Muhamad Asad and developing a series of books on Islamic education. In 2009 and subsequent years Kabir was named as one of the "500 Most Influential Muslims in the World". He has toured North America as Shaikh with the Whirling Dervishes of Turkey, bringing Sufi culture to more than 100,000 people.

The focus of his work is on contributing to a new language of spirituality to express the fundamental psychological and meta-physical truths of the spiritual process. His books on spirituality, *Living Presence* and *The Knowing Heart,* have been published in at least eight languages. Among his recent publications are:

Love's Ripening, Rumi on the Heart's Journey; and *The Rumi Daybook*. In 2017 a 25th anniversary commemorative edition of the classic, *Living Presence*, is to be published by Tarcher Penguin in their 'Spiritual Cornerstones' series.

Kabir regularly writes articles and blogs for *The Huffington Post*, *Tikkun*, patheos.com, and *The Times of India*.

Anodea Judith

Anodea Judith, PhD, is the author of many bestselling books on spirituality, psychology and social change. She holds a doctorate in health and human services, with a speciality in mind–body healing, and a Master's in clinical psychology. Her books on the chakra system, marrying Eastern and Western disciplines, considered groundbreaking in the field of transpersonal psychology, are used as definitive texts in the US and elsewhere. With a million books in print in 14 languages, she has won a reputation for solid scholarship. She also has international renown as a dynamic speaker and workshop leader. She is the founder and director of Sacred Centers, a teaching organization that offers workshops and teleclasses in chakras, evolutionary activism, yoga, manifestation techniques and much more (see www.sacredcenters.com). Her book *The Global Heart Awakens*, which charts the movement from the love of power to the power of love, won two literary awards. She teaches and lectures worldwide.

Ervin László

Twice nominated for the Nobel Peace Prize, Ervin László received the Goi Peace Prize in 2001. He has written more than 70 books, which have been translated into 20 languages, and has published more than 400 articles and research papers.

His work in recent years has focused on the "Akasha Paradigm", the new conception of cosmos, life and conscious-ness emerging at the forefront of the contemporary sciences. He serves as President of the Club of Budapest, Chairman of the Ervin László Center for Advanced Study, Chancellor of the Giordano Bruno New-Paradigm University, and Editor of *World Futures: The Journal of New Paradigm Research.*

He is recipient of the highest degree in philosophy and human sciences from the Sorbonne, the University of Paris, as well as of the coveted Artist Diploma of the Liszt Ferenc Academy of Budapest. Additional prizes and awards include four honorary doctorates. He is an adviser to the UNESCO Director General, ambassador of the International Delphic Council, and member of the World Academy of Art and Science and the International Academy of Philosophy.

Barbara Marx Hubbard

As a prolific author and educator, Barbara has written seven books on social and planetary evolution. She has produced, hosted and contributed to many documentaries seen by millions of people around the world.

In 1984 she was nominated for the Vice Presidency of the United States on the Democratic ticket. She called for a "Peace Room" to scan for, map, connect and communicate what is working in America and the world. She co-founded the World Future Society, the Association for Global New Thought and the Foundation for Conscious Evolution.

Her books are: *The Hunger of Eve: One Woman's Odyssey toward the Future*; *The Evolutionary Journey: Your Guide to a Positive Future*; *Revelation: Our Crisis is a Birth – An Evolutionary Interpretation of the New Testament*; *Conscious Evolution: Awakening the Power of Our Social Potential*; *Emergence: The Shift from Ego to Essence*; *52 Codes for Conscious Self Evolution* and *Birth 2012 and Beyond: Humanity's Great Shift to the Age of Conscious Evolution.*

Mona Polacca

Mona Polacca is a Havasupai, Hopi and Tewa Native American whose tribal affiliation is with the Colorado River Indian Tribes of Parker, Arizona. A recognized wisdom carrier, she is a member of the International Council of Thirteen Indigenous Grandmothers, a group of women representing indigenous cultures from around the world who are concerned about threats to the Earth and to indigenous ways of life. The Council has travelled extensively and presented at major conferences across the planet. Mona is also featured in a collection of teachings and stories compiled in the book *Grandmothers Counsel the World: Women Elders Offer Their Vision for Our Planet.*

Michael A Singer

Michael A Singer is the author of the *New York Times* best-sellers *The Untethered Soul* and *The Surrender Experiment*. He had a deep inner awakening in 1971 while working on his doctorate in economics and went into seclusion to focus on yoga and meditation. The long-established Temple of the Universe, which he founded in 1975, is a yoga and meditation centre where people of any religion or belief system can come together to experience inner peace. He is also the creator of a leading-edge software package that transformed the medical practice management industry, and he is founding CEO of a billion-dollar public company whose achievements are archived in the Smithsonian Institution. Along with more than four decades of spiritual teaching, Michael has made major contributions in business, education, healthcare and environmental protection.